Adolescent Brain Development
Implications for Behavior

Michelle K. Jetha, Ph.D.
Sidney J. Segalowitz, Ph.D.

AMSTERDAM • BOSTON • HEIDELBERG • LONDON
NEW YORK • OXFORD • PARIS • SAN DIEGO
SAN FRANCISCO • SINGAPORE • SYDNEY • TOKYO
Academic Press is an imprint of Elsevier

Academic Press is an imprint of Elsevier
The Boulevard, Langford Lane, Kidlington, Oxford, OX5 1GB, UK
225 Wyman Street, Waltham, MA 02451, USA

First published 2012. Transferred to Digital Printing, 2012.

British Library Cataloguing in Publication Data
A catalogue record for this book is available from the British Library

Library of Congress Cataloging-in-Publication Data
A catalog record for this book is available from the Library of Congress

ISBN: 978-0-12-397916-2

For information on all Academic Press publications
visit our website at *store.elsevier.com*

This book has been manufactured using Print On Demand technology. Each copy is produced to order
and is limited to black ink. The online version of this book will show color figures where appropriate.

Printed in the United States of America.

#8183l6837

TABLE OF CONTENTS

Preface... v

Introduction... vii

**Chapter 1 Structural Brain Development in Late Childhood,
Adolescence, and Early Adulthood**....................... 1

1.1 Introduction... 1

1.2 Anatomical Changes.. 3

1.3 Summary.. 17

Chapter 2 Connectivity... 19

2.1 Changes in Networks Over Childhood, Adolescence,
and Young Adulthood.. 19

2.2 How are Changes in Connectivity Related to
Development in the Cognitive Domain?...................... 21

2.3 Implications.. 24

Chapter 3 Social and Emotional Development................... 25

3.1 The Development of Social Information Processing......... 26

3.2 Models of Social Behavior.. 37

3.3 Aggression... 45

3.4 Individual Differences in Social Behavior:
A Personality Perspective.. 47

**Chapter 4 How Genes and Environment Work Together
to Influence Brain Growth and Behavior**............. 53

4.1 Genetic Effects on Brain Growth............................... 53

4.2 A Broad Range of Experiential Factors Influence Brain
Development... 62

4.3 Implications: The Bottom Line.................................. 69

Summary and Implications.. 71

References.. 81

PREFACE

It is hard to exaggerate the degree to which research over the past two decades has been energized by the realization that adolescent brain growth is dynamic. A simple search of a leading online database (PubMed) with the code words "brain development" and "adolescence" yields over 5,000 refereed journal articles since the year 2000. In the past 20 years, social psychologists and neuroscientists have started to collaborate in a way that would have seemed, before this period, impossible or pointless. Before this time, their worldviews on how the mind works differed so much that such collaboration would have more likely ended in frustration than in fruitful scholarship. Today, through collaborative efforts and facilitated by new technologies, the field of developmental social neuroscience is well established and is grounded on the premise that the full understanding of social development can only come from the integration of multiple levels of analyses. We now have numerous journals whose titles include various combinations of social, cognitive, affective, and developmental neuroscience, with a great deal of emphasis on the adolescent period. It is a terrifically exciting time to be in this field.

In December of 2010, we were asked by the Ontario Ministry of Child and Youth Services to summarize and synthesize the research literature on adolescent brain development and the implications of this development for behavior, including the potential implications for public policies that concern adolescent welfare. We completed this project in April 2011 and have continued to think about the challenges that this task presented to us.

Pulling this broad field together has been useful to our own thinking concerning our research and teaching, and we have continued to find new research to add to our synthesis. As we gave community talks on the topic, we identified gaps in the published literature of material that was devoted to translating empirical research to a more readable form for individuals who are working with young people. This was not surprising considering how rapidly the field is advancing. On numerous occasions, we were asked to produce a readable, brief summary of research in the field, so that these findings would be readily available to healthcare practitioners, community workers, and parents. The requests also came from college and university instructors who wanted this information summarized in what could be a supplementary text, one that not only links the research to real-world issues but also provides the reader with some sense of the controversies in the field. With this online book, we have attempted to fill this gap. We aimed to provide an accessible overview of brain changes from childhood through adolescence and early adulthood with an emphasis on the implications for social and emotional behavior. We hope that our brief coverage of this biological perspective will shed new light for our readers on this creative, passionate, and often tumultuous period of development.

Integrating the research in the field has been a rewarding challenge. We would like to especially thank Allison Flynn Bowman for her invaluable help in searching out sources and arranging permissions for reproduction of figures. We would also like to thank the Ontario Ministry of Child and Youth Services for getting us started on this venture and giving us a free hand to deal with the task as we saw fit.

Michelle K. Jetha, Ph.D.
Sidney J. Segalowitz, Ph.D.
April 2012

INTRODUCTION

"There's been a great deal of emphasis in the 1990s on the critical importance of the first three years. I certainly applaud those efforts. But what happens sometimes when an area is emphasized so much is other areas are forgotten. And even though the first 3 years are important, so are the next 16. And the ages between 3 and 16, there's still enormous dynamic activity happening in brain biology. I think that that might have been somewhat overlooked with the emphasis on the early years."

**Jay Giedd-Chief, Unit on Brain Imaging,
Child Psychiatry Branch, NIMH**[106]

As recently as the mid 1990s, the prevailing notion among neuroscientists was that the most important aspect of brain development ended by about 3 years of age. This assumption led to an explosion of research on early brain maturation with an emphasis on early life experiences, the importance of gene and environment interactions, and the central role of early relationships with caregivers. Since that time, with the advent of new imaging technologies and the work of developmental neuroscientists, we now know that the brain continues to organize, adapt, and change well beyond the early years, and, in some respects, over the full lifespan. The physical changes in the brain that occur during late childhood, adolescence, and into young adulthood are particularly dramatic and occur at all levels: molecular, cellular, anatomical, and functional.

These physical changes are accompanied by notable changes in social behavior. For example, preteens transition from being more dependent on caregivers to becoming independent young adults. There is also a shift from more family-oriented to more peer-oriented interactions, and an increase in the appeal of novelty and excitement, and the desire to explore and take risks. Such transitions are healthy and lead to opportunities to hone important social and behavioral skills that will be necessary for taking on adult roles and responsibilities. Unfortunately, they may also come with a cost.

Adolescence is a time of increased drug use and unprotected sex, and the three highest causes of mortality in adolescents are accidents, homicides, and suicides.[143]

This developmental period is also marked by variations in emotionality and in self-regulation. In adolescence, emotions become more intense, fluctuate more often and are more subject to extremes than those experienced by children and adults. Concurrent with these emotional changes are shifts in behavioral regulation. In childhood, behavioral regulation is more externally derived from the guidance and constraints put in place by parents and caregivers, whereas in adolescence there is an increasing need for self-regulation. The way in which changes in emotionality and self-regulation are negotiated will greatly influence how well the adolescent navigates through his/her expanding social world. How effectively preteens and adolescents learn to self-regulate impulses and emotions will influence not only decisions about participation in dangerous activities, but also vulnerability to psychopathology. This is especially important considering that the lifetime risk for the emergence of psychopathology peaks at age 14.[152]

During the past 20 years, studies have accumulated that document the physical brain changes during the transition from childhood to adulthood, whereas numerous others have begun to pave the way for a more in-depth understanding of the functional significance of these changes. Can we explain notable social and emotional changes from a brain-based perspective? In the following chapters, we will provide a summary of findings from this exciting frontier in brain research. After a description of the dramatic changes in brain structure and connectivity over this period, we turn our attention to how such changes may influence social and emotional maturation. We conclude with a discussion of genetic and environmental factors that contribute to individual differences in behavioral outcomes.

CHAPTER *1*

Structural Brain Development in Late Childhood, Adolescence, and Early Adulthood

1.1 INTRODUCTION

The brain, like all bodily structures, goes through a very high rate of growth prenatally and in the early years after birth. However, research has demonstrated that this development spans well into young adulthood and is more protracted than was realized even just a couple of decades ago. The physical changes in gray matter, white matter, and neurotransmitters from late childhood to early adulthood are dramatic and have implications for understanding changes in behavior during this period. They are both progressive (building up) and regressive (reducing and fine tuning) and are sensitive to maturational and environmental influences (see Box 1.1). In this chapter, we provide a general overview of these changes.

BOX 1.1 Progressive and Regressive Changes in the Brain

Progressive changes include proliferation of neurons (neurogenesis) and synapses (synaptogenesis), and growth of myelin (myelination).

Regressive changes include cell death and synaptic pruning, both presumably related to usage (the "Use it or lose it" principle).

The triggers for synaptic function are neurotransmitters (such as dopamine, serotonin, norepinephrine, and GABA), which follow their own growth and decline cycles.

1.1.1 The Early Years...

It is well known that the early years are marked by critical periods of brain development. There are billions of neurons in the brain that send messages to one another across synapses (see Figure 1.1) and allow the various regions of the brain to function in a coordinated way. Early in life there is a dramatic period of *synaptogenesis* that results in an overproduction of synapses, which is followed by a "competition" among neurons and synapses (see Box 1.2). Animal studies have demonstrated that the

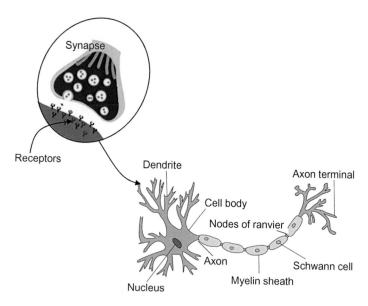

Fig. 1.1. Schematic of the neuron and synapse. The synapse is the junction that permits one neuron's axon to pass a signal to the receiving neuron's dendrite. (See Plate 1).

BOX 1.2 Early Neural Development

Neural development begins two weeks after conception with the formation of the *neural tube* (which will become the brain and spinal cord), *neuronal proliferation* (the few initial cells will continually divide to produce billions of neurons), *neural migration* (cells migrate to their final destination) and *neural differentiation* (cells differentiate to become specialized for particular functions).

During the process of neuronal proliferation (mostly completed between the 4th and 7th months of gestation), many more neurons are created than will ultimately be used and maintained.

As neurons complete their migration, they extend axons and dendrites to create synaptic connections. This process is referred to as *synaptogenesis* and accounts for the connections between neuronal cells (see Figure 1.1).

In early childhood, there is a dramatic period of synaptogenesis that results in an overproduction of synapses, which is followed by a competition among neurons and synapses for *neural growth factors*, which support cell function. Neurons that receive support will be maintained, while those that do not will die through the process called *apoptosis*.

strengthening or elimination of neurons is dependent on environmental demands and experience; those that are more often used are strengthened, whereas those that are rarely used are eliminated. The process of "weeding out" weaker synapses is known as *synaptic pruning* and is thought to result in a brain that is more efficient and matches neural connectivity to need.[216] Thus, early brain development (birth to 6 years) is an extraordinary time of brain plasticity, where environmental enrichment and deprivation play a major role in shaping and molding the brain for the years to come.

1.1.2 After the Age of Seven…

Although brain volume is about 90% of its adult size by 6 years of age and reaches its adult size by about the age of 12,[201] brain development is far from complete. With the advent of new technologies, such as magnetic resonance imaging (MRI), we now know that the brain continues to develop and change throughout the lifespan, although at a slower pace than during the early years. There is a notable surge of synapse growth just before the onset of puberty[111] and another prominent period of synaptic pruning and plasticity during the adolescent period. In some brain regions, up to half of the synaptic connections are eliminated.[216,282] This second period of substantial synaptic pruning (the first being during the early years) is thought to contribute to the refinement of brain connectivity that is necessary for the emergence of adult brain circuitry (see Chapter 2). Indeed, it has become well accepted in recent years that adolescence encompasses an important period of brain development that is sensitive to the environment in terms of learning and experience, and as such has become the focus of an increasing amount of research.

1.2 ANATOMICAL CHANGES

Brain maturation over this period, which includes the remodeling and fine-tuning of neural circuitry, does not occur in a linear and uniform pattern. It is specific with respect to brain region, timing, and gender. Before considering these important changes, let us first turn our attention to a brief overview of brain anatomy.

The organization of the brain is, in some respects, analogous to the components of a computer. The surface gray matter is where the brain "processing" takes place, whereas the white matter provides the connectivity or "wiring" between regions. The brain as a whole is divided into two halves, the left and right cerebral hemispheres. Each cerebral hemisphere consists

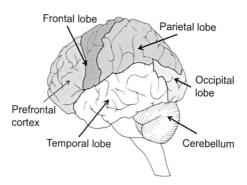

Fig. 1.2. Schematic of the lateral surface of the brain. The surface gray matter of the lobes comprises the cortex, consisting of the four lobes, with the prefrontal subdivision of the frontal lobe colored in light yellow. The cerebellum is considered to be one of many subcortical structures (i.e., gray matter below the cortex). (See Plate 2).

of surface gray matter (the cortex), inner white matter, and a number of gray matter subcortical regions (see Figure 1.9).

Surface gray matter can be further divided into four lobes (see Figure 1.2). The *frontal lobe* is comprised of the motor cortex, which is central to voluntary movement, and the prefrontal region, which is central to higher-order thinking and executive functions such as strategizing and planning. The parietal lobe primarily serves the functions of touch sensation and spatial thinking. The temporal lobe is involved in language reception, auditory perception, memory, and a number of social cognitive functions. The occipital lobe is central to vision.

Higher-order functions are mediated by subdivisions of the *prefrontal cortex* (see Figure 1.3) which work together to subserve complex attention, monitoring of the environment and of the self, and emotional and behavioral control. As we will discuss, several of these prefrontal subdivisions, especially those in the *medial prefrontal* regions, have been implicated in social and emotional developments.

The *white matter* of the brain is made up of the axons that emanate from the cell bodies to send signals to other cells. These axons are insulated by *myelin*, a sheath that surrounds the axons and promotes signal transmission (see Figure 1.1). White matter is responsible for connectivity, linking brain regions that are far apart or close together. The largest white matter tract is the *corpus callosum*, which has the primary function of transferring information between left and right cerebral hemispheres (see Figure 1.4).

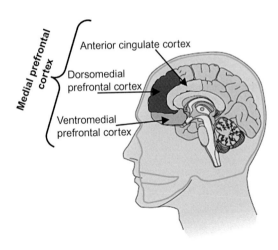

Fig. 1.3. Schematic of the medial (inside) view of the brain. This view shows the divisions of the medial prefrontal cortex and the anterior cingulate. (See Plate 3).

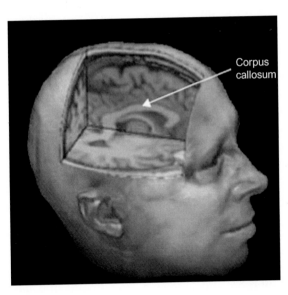

Fig. 1.4. The corpus callosum is the largest structure of axonal tracts in the brain (approximately 200 million nerve fibers), facilitating interhemispheric communication and influencing language learning and associative thinking. The area of the corpus callosum increases robustly from ages 4 to 22 years. (Source: See Ref. 9.) (See Plate 4).

1.2.1 Gray Matter

Imaging studies of the human brain have demonstrated that the volume of cortical gray matter follows an inverted U-shaped trajectory across development. During childhood, regional gray matter "thickens" or increases in volume, peaks in late childhood or early adolescence, and

BOX 1.3 Estimates of the Ages of Peak Thickening of the Cortex

Region	Functions	Girls/Boys
Frontal lobes	Planning, organizing, strategizing, initiating, shifting, sustaining attention	11.0 years/12.1 years
Temporal lobes	Language, emotion, memory	16.7 years/16.2 years
Parietal lobes	Receiving and processing sensory input	10.2 years/11.8 years

Data from a study of 145 healthy participants from ages 4 to 21 years.[109]

then begins to "thin" or decline in volume into early adulthood. The thickening is thought to be primarily due to an increase in the number and thickness of branches and connections on the dendrites and axons of the existing neurons, referred to as *arborization*. A notable surge in thickening occurs just before the onset of puberty (at 11 years in girls and 12 years in boys, on average).[111] However, the age at which the thickening of gray matter peaks differs according to brain region and by gender (see Box 1.3).

The thinning of gray matter results from several factors. These include the pruning of synapses, axons, and dendrites, a reduction in neuronal support cells (*glial cells*), and myelination that increases white matter relative to the gray matter volume.[203,234,260] The decline or thinning in regional gray matter volume is viewed as a reliable marker of maturation, a period of shaping and "rewiring" of the synapses that is sensitive to environmental influences (see Figure 1.5). This process is assumed to be responsible for 40% of the reduction of synapses during adolescence.[139,216]

Overall, gray matter maturation proceeds in a back-to-front direction, occurring first in areas toward the back of the brain that receive information from the senses (vision, hearing, and touch), then in regions involved in spatial orientation and language, and finally in regions with more advanced functioning such as those that integrate sensory information coming from multiple brain regions. These higher-order cortical regions of integration are called *association regions* (see Figure 1.6). Association regions located in the frontal lobes, for example, the lateral prefrontal cortices, are among the last to mature during adolescence.[114,240,260] These regions are involved in the higher-order integration of information such as planning, strategizing, and goal setting that require the ability to allocate attention and control impulses. The temporal poles, association

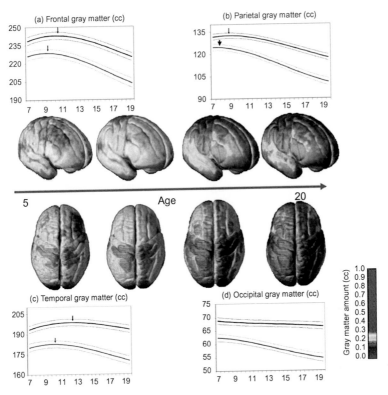

Fig. 1.5. Cortical gray matter development in healthy children between 4 and 22 years of age rescanned every 2 years. The brain images are of the right lateral and top views showing thickening and thinning of gray matter over maturation. Cortical gray matter appears to progress in a "back-to-front" manner. The color bar indicates the amount of gray matter (red-pink: more grey matter; blue-purple: gray matter loss). The graphs show total lobar volumes in male (blue) and female (red) healthy children aged 7 to 20 years. Arrows indicate peak gray matter volume for each curve, and dotted lines represent the confidence intervals. (Source: See Ref. 115.) (See Plate 5).

regions situated between the temporal and frontal lobes of the brain, integrate sensory information with motivational and emotional information. These regions are not fully mature until adulthood.[110,114,193] There are some exceptions to this pattern of cortical thinning over development, but it holds for much of the cortex.[240,241]

It is important to note that maturation in several brain areas has been related to measures of performance. For example, maturation in the prefrontal cortex has been related to intelligence[233] and impulse control[45] over childhood and adolescence. Similarly, research suggests that maturation in motor brain regions is related to measures of fine motor skills, whereas maturation in left hemisphere areas is related to increased language processing skills.[166,242]

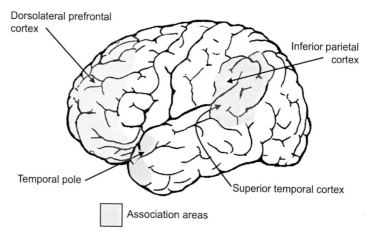

Fig. 1.6. Association cortex regions with specific subregions labeled. The association areas integrate information from multiple brain regions. (See Plate 6).

1.2.2 White Matter

White matter volume begins to increase early in the postnatal period and continues over childhood, adolescence, and into middle adulthood, with some studies showing peak volume in the middle of the fifth decade of life.[20,201,276] The organization of white matter, including changes in its microstructure, can now be visualized in brain images using a technique called diffusion tensor imaging (DTI).[17] (See Figure 1.7. Note that the white matter is colored so as to illustrate the separate pathways.) In contrast to findings that suggest a linear pattern of maturation for white matter development, research using DTI has demonstrated that microstructural organization occurs well into the second decade of life followed by a steady decline after 30 years of age.[142,161]

The maturation of white matter organization proceeds at different rates in different regions.[7,262] Some regions are mature by adolescence and others are still maturing into young adulthood, particularly those linking the frontal and parietal regions (see Figures 1.8, (I) and (II)).[7,18,188] Just as with the development of gray matter, the development of white matter is protracted in regions that support complex behavior and cognition. We can delineate three stages of white matter development with specific white matter tracts developing before, during, and after adolescence.[7] Importantly, the tracts that are undergoing substantial maturation during the adolescent period are involved in emotional, behavioral, and cognitive control, such as those connecting subcortical regions (e.g., basal ganglia, see Figure 1.9) with

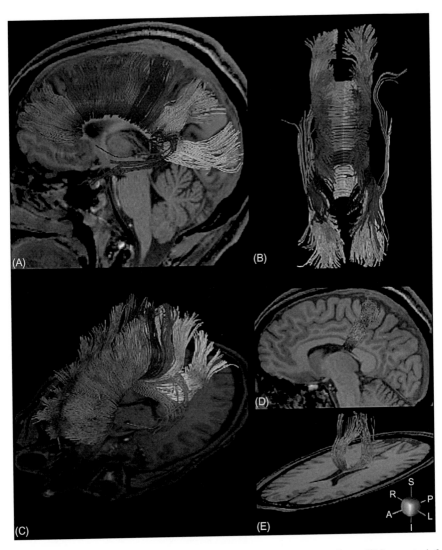

Fig. 1.7. Different views (using DTI) of the fiber tracts running through the brain as a sort of 'internal highway system' of the cortex. All fibers here connect the hemispheres through the corpus callosum, and then turn upward on both sides. (A) Side view, showing fibers sweeping upward in the medial side of the right hemisphere, in prefrontal (green), premotor (light blue), motor (dark blue), parietal (orange), and occipital (yellow) cortex, and between the left and right temporal lobes (violet). (B) The view of the fibers from front (green) to back (yellow). (C) The side view seen from the top. (D) and (E) Two more views of callosal fibers projecting into primary motor cortex. (Source: See Ref. 136.) (See Plate 7).

prefrontal regions.[13,165] This age-related pattern has implications for learning. Region-specific maturation of white matter over childhood and adolescence correlates with intelligence,[227,233] reading skills,[189,212] visuospatial skills,[99,173] language[8] response inhibition,[173,255] and memory.[172]

(I) Mature by adolescence

Association tracts

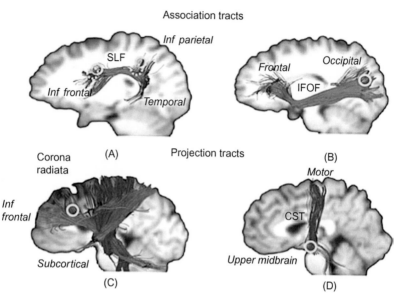

Projection tracts

Corona radiata   (A)

(B)

Inf frontal

Subcortical

(C)

Motor

CST

Upper midbrain

(D)

(II) Still immature during adolescence

Association tracts   Interhemispheric tract

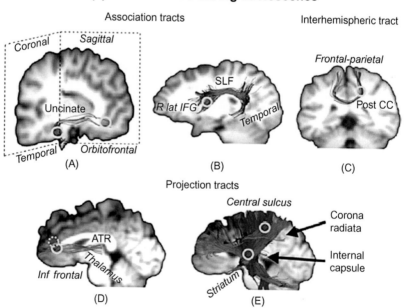

(A)   (B)   (C)

Projection tracts

(D)   (E)

Fig. 1.8. (I) White matter tracts that are mature by ages 8–12. These are broadly distributed neural networks. (II) White matter tracts that are still maturing in 13–17 year olds. Some of these support top-down executive control over behavior, and some integrate information by communicating between the two hemispheres. (Source: See Ref. 7, reproduced with permission.) (See Plate 8).

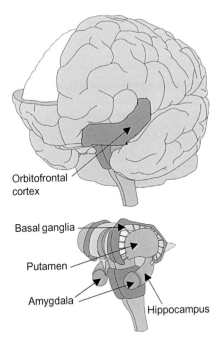

Fig. 1.9. An illustration of how subcortical regions, including the basal ganglia, putamen, amygdala, and hippocampus are tucked inside the cerebral hemispheres. (Source: See Ref. 9.) (See Plate 9).

The largest white matter tract is the *corpus callosum* (see Figure 1.4). As mentioned above, it allows for integration of information across the two sides of the brain. It thickens considerably from 4 to 22 years, and changes in thickness have been related to intelligence, although the relations vary with gender and age.[168]

The findings of DTI studies reflect in part the maturation of myelin. As indicated earlier, the development of myelin promotes signal transmission. Myelination increases the speed of communication between neurons and is important for the timing and synchrony of neuronal firing between distant brain regions.[113,237] This process was previously thought to be a genetically determined static structure. However, it is now known that myelination is a dynamic and experience-dependent process. One important aspect of myelination is that it actually limits the brain's ability to adapt. As myelin develops, it inhibits axon sprouting and the creation of new synapses that are characteristic of growth and adaptability. As a result, the completion of myelination limits environmentally-induced changes in connectivity. So, while making transmission more efficient, it limits further developmental changes, leading to region-specific windows of time when experience can influence changes in connectivity.[a,95,96]

Considerable changes in myelination take place from childhood to adolescence.[19] For example, increased myelin content in the tract joining regions involved in emotion control (cingulate) and memory (hippocampus) doubles during the teenage years. A functional benefit of this slow development is that the brain has time to "wire" according to experience.

1.2.3 Experience-Induced Changes in Both Gray and White Matter

In addition to the accumulation of studies that document structural changes in both gray and white matter over development, researchers have also examined experience-induced changes in gray and white matter. For example, practice in specific skills has been shown to increase gray matter size, as shown in studies assessing the effect on the brain of violin playing and juggling practice.[34,81,87,197,198] Experience through training and level of skill, such as in piano playing, juggling, and spatial working memory, has also been shown to lead to structural changes in white matter density.[21,228,259] Other studies show relations suggestive of (or at least consistent with) experience-induced changes, such as the relations between corpus callosum thickness and the degree of bimanual coordination skill.[145] Conversely, a lack of environmental input may also limit growth. Studies have reported that the brains of children who have been severely neglected show a reduction of white matter density in some structures compared with those children who have not experienced neglect.[265]

We must keep in mind that experience-induced changes in gray and white matter are not independent, as they are connected in terms of functional activation. With new imaging technologies, we are now starting to understand how brain maturation is a result of a dynamic interplay between biologically driven growth processes, environmental influences and experiences, as well as the functional connectivity between regions (see Chapter 2).

1.2.4 Subcortical Maturation

Until the 1990s, it was generally thought that the cortex was still slowly maturing into the early years, but that the subcortical structures

---

[a]Plasticity is not entirely disrupted by this process as some portions remain unmyelinated, and therefore the brain retains some plasticity right into older adulthood.[164]

(see Figure 1.9) that serve more basic functions were fully mature at birth. The circumstantial evidence for this assumption was that although some cortical damage at birth or in infancy could result in reorganization of functions and virtually complete recovery of function, such early damage to subcortical regions rarely permitted such plasticity. Thus, neurologists concluded that the subcortex was more complete and "fixed" by infancy. It turns out this was naïve and wrong as well.

Subcortical gray matter thins just as the cortical gray matter, although to a lesser degree.[107,112] The subcortical region supports many functions, an important set of which includes arousal and the automatic processing of emotion, commonly called "gut" responses. As we will discuss in the chapter on connectivity, the pathways connecting these subcortical regions to the prefrontal cortex change over adolescence in a way that reflects increased top–down control from prefrontal regions. Stimuli that would have previously evoked relatively automatic behavioral responses and emotional arousal come under greater control through the planning and reasoning skills associated with the prefrontal cortex. Such changes are thought to lead to emotional maturity, including the ability to regulate and interpret emotions.

One subcortical region involved in the control of movement and muscle tone and more recently shown to be involved in attention and emotional states is the *basal ganglia* (see Box 1.4). One of its subregions (the caudate nucleus) is a relay station for information that will be sent to the prefrontal cortex, and it also follows an inverted U-shaped trajectory of growth, peaking earlier in girls than in boys (7.5 years in girls and 10 years in boys).[109] This subregion is involved in making certain behavioral routines more versus less automatic.[134] Other subregions involved in action selection and in the reward system also reach peak gray matter volumes in early adolescence and then show a decline in volume into adulthood.[165,195,243]

BOX 1.4 The Basal Ganglia

This subcortical region includes several subregions: caudate nucleus, putamen, globus pallidus, subthalamic nucleus, substantia nigra, and ventral striatum (which includes the nucleus accumbens and the olfactory tubercle). It is central to physical factors such the control of movement and muscle tone, but is involved also in attention and emotional states.

Another key subcortical structure is the *amygdala*. It is involved with the processing of emotions, and has been implicated in disorders of emotion dysregulation, such as aggressive behavior, depression, and anxiety. This region increases over adolescence and young adulthood, and does so more sharply for males than for females.[111,112,195] Such changes may be related to research showing that adolescents show increased reactivity in the amygdala when responding to emotional stimuli compared with adults.[127]

The *hippocampus* is another gray matter subcortical structure situated next to the amygdala. It is central to many functions needed for normal psychological functioning, including memory storage and retrieval. Memory is one of the functions that improve significantly over childhood and through adolescence, as is apparent from educational challenges. This region also increases in size over adolescence and young adulthood, more robustly for females than for males.[111,112,195] The hippocampus experiences important changes during adolescence in its synaptic organization, dopamine circuitry (see neurotransmitter section below), and myelination.[18] Although the amygdala and hippocampus regions both show increases in gray matter into adulthood, the rate of this change begins to slow down after early adolescence, suggesting that the maturation of these areas is mostly complete by this time.[195]

The *cerebellum* is another structure critical for normal functioning (see Figure 1.2). It has long been known to be centrally involved in the coordination of movement, but more recently, we have come to realize that it is also associated with higher cognitive functions such as language and emotional control. The cerebellum is larger in males than females over childhood and adolescence, but these differences diminish in adulthood.[266] The growth of the outer region of the cerebellum follows an inverted U-shaped growth trajectory, peaking at 11.3 years in girls and 15.6 years in boys, and the thinning also occurs earlier in females.[48] The growth rate differences during adolescence may be due to sex differences in genes and pubertal hormones. Abnormalities in the cerebellum have been consistently reported in individuals with autism and attention deficit hyperactivity disorder (ADHD). Compared to other areas of the brain, cerebellum volume increases relatively late in gestation, and thus may be particularly vulnerable to environmental influences such as oxygen deprivation, toxins, or other environmental factors.[60]

1.2.5 Efficiency and Brain Metabolism

It is costly in terms of energy to maintain excess neurons and synapses. In fact, brain metabolism rises during early childhood until roughly 3–4 years of age, stays at that level, and then begins to show regional declines around 9–10 years of age, reaching adult levels of metabolism by around 16–18 years.[58,59,78] It is not a coincidence that this schedule resembles the pattern of cortical thinning. Such changes likely reflect the more efficient processing of information that occurs with the organization and myelination of white matter.[78,159] Together, the thinning of gray matter, the maturation of white matter and the decline in metabolism contribute to more efficient brain processing.

1.2.6 Sex Differences in Brain Maturation

Puberty is a stage of adolescence involving a cascade of hormonal changes that lead to reproductive maturation. These hormonal changes affect both brain activity and its organization.

Total brain volume is approximately 10% larger for males than females throughout childhood and adolescence, a difference not related to body size or weight. The difference in brain size between the sexes does not influence the degree of connectivity or receptor density, or other factors related to brain functional capacity, and thus does not translate into functional differences.[111] In general, studies have found that when controlling for differences in brain size between the sexes, males have a greater proportion of white matter than females, and females have a greater proportion of gray matter.[3,122] The functional relevance of these differences is not well understood. More recent evidence is accumulating to suggest that the pattern of white matter development may also differ between the sexes; although males show more rapid white matter growth, females show earlier maturation of white matter structure.[7,125]

Several differences in the sizes of brain regions have been noted (see Box 1.5). Across the adolescent period, the amygdala increases significantly in boys, although the hippocampus volume increases in girls.[111] Hormone surges are thought to influence differential brain growth in these regions because the amygdala has a high number of androgen receptors,[62] and the hippocampus has a high number of estrogen receptors.[185]

> ## BOX 1.5 Pubertal Hormones and Brain Growth
>
> The onset of puberty begins with the secretion of gonadotropin releasing hormone, which triggers a cascade resulting in sex hormone production. These hormones affect the brain's activation, its organization, and its mechanisms of growth. For example, luteinizing hormone has been related to increased white matter content[205] and testosterone may affect the diameter of the axon.[206] The rise in gonadal hormones between 10 and 15 years has been associated with declines in gray matter in several cortical regions among girls, although not in boys.[204]
>
> Sex hormone receptors are plentiful in the amygdala and hippocampus, and such receptor differences may be responsible for differences in regional growth patterns between boys and girls.
>
> Other regions that may be affected include regions that differ in size between the sexes. On average, male children and adolescents have larger amygdala and globus pallidus sizes than females,[48,217] whereas females have larger caudate nuclei and cingulate gyrus volumes compared to males.[48,108,280]

The growth rate of gray matter regions also differs for boys and girls (see Figure 1.4 and Box 1.3). Gray matter volume in the frontal and parietal lobes peaks approximately one year earlier in girls (11 years) compared with boys (12 years),[109] which parallels the 1-year delay in the average onset of puberty for boys (mean age of 12 years) compared with girls (mean age of 11 years). Paus and colleagues[202] have also reported sex differences in white matter development during adolescence. Females showed little change between 12 and 18 years of age, whereas males showed dramatic changes during this period, much of which was accounted for by changes in testosterone levels.

The differential trajectories may have implications for differences in risk for psychopathology between the sexes during this period. For example, the rate of depression for boys and girls is equal prior to puberty, but changes to an increased prevalence (2:1) for girls over boys after puberty. Indeed, stage of puberty is a better predictor of gender differences in rates of depression than is chronological age.[130,199]

1.2.7 Neurotransmitter Systems

Neurotransmitters are chemicals that have important functions in the brain. All neurotransmitters transmit signals from one neuron to the next across synapses. The neurotransmitters are either characterized as excitatory or inhibitory depending on whether they increase or decrease the likelihood of signal transmisison. Dopamine is especially important in the context of brain development because of the abundance of receptors for dopamine in the synapses of the reward system and in areas central to executive functions (the prefrontal regions) (see Box 1.6).

BOX 1.6 Dopamine and the Reward System

Dopamine is an important neurotransmitter that is involved in the brain's response to reward. In fact, dopamine neurons are one of the primary inputs to reward regions of the brain and are thought to influence learning about what is rewarding in the environment. The dopamine system undergoes elaborate changes over the adolescent period that are thought to increase the appeal and learning of reward during this time.[246,275]

Most of what is known about changes in the dopamine system over development has been obtained from animal studies due to limitations in measuring such chemical activity in human brains. The results from animal studies are clear: dopamine projections from the prefrontal cortex to subcortical regions increase from adolescence to adulthood.[4,264] In humans, the regional changes in the efficiency of dopamine receptors over adolescence and into adulthood follow the maturational pattern of the prefrontal cortex.[147] Changes during adolescence in dopamine pathways and receptor function have implications for incentive motivation (i.e., reward motivation) and behavior, particularly risk-taking behaviors (see Chapter 3).

1.3 SUMMARY

The structural brain changes that occur over late childhood, adolescence, and into young adulthood are particularly dramatic. Overall, gray matter development follows an inverted U-pattern of growth, first thickening in volume, peaking, and then thinning. White matter increases in a roughly linear pattern over this time. The process of myelination, which speeds up the communication between nerve cells in the brain, also serves to limit plasticity, leading to windows of time during development when experience can affect changes in connectivity. Gray matter and white matter maturation proceed in a back-to-front manner, first in brain regions underlying sensory systems and movement and lastly in regions that integrate this information, such as the frontal regions involved in planning, strategizing, and goal setting. These changes are experience-dependent and lead to a brain that is more economical and more efficient, a brain that is wired and tuned for adult activities.

CHAPTER 2

Connectivity

Advances in imaging technology have led to new conceptualizations regarding the development of the brain. We now realize that brain maturation does not occur in stages mapped onto the development of specific regions, but rather it is dependent on the emergence of large-scale "networks." Networks consist of brain regions that activate or work together through their interconnections. The gray and white matter changes discussed in Chapter 1, such as synaptic pruning and myelination, play important roles in their development. It is the development and formation of networks that provides the physiological basis for the sophisticated processing that occurs as the brain matures. Such changes serve to reorganize, rebalance, and fine-tune the "neural circuitry" of the brain in ways that lead to more efficient and controlled information processing and more complex cognitive functioning. With new technologies, neuroscientists are increasingly able to map the maturation of these networks.

2.1 CHANGES IN NETWORKS OVER CHILDHOOD, ADOLESCENCE, AND YOUNG ADULTHOOD

Over childhood, adolescence, and young adulthood, many of the connections between brain regions show dramatic changes.[93,152,258,270] These changes lead to processing that is more specialized and efficient. Two main findings have consistently been reported when participants are at rest and/or when they are performing specific tasks:

1. Cortical connections change from being more nonspecific and spread out to being more focused. This is illustrated in Figure 2.1, which shows brain activity during a task that is designed to engage prefrontal areas. As can be seen, the activation of the prefrontal areas in childhood (7–12 years) covers a larger area (i.e., is more spread out) than in adolescents and adults. In childhood, brain activation during cognitive processing is relatively nonspecific, producing coactivation of regions that are anatomically close together. As the networks mature, this activation becomes more focused and specialized.[92,93] Such changes in cortical activation over development coincide with the maturation of gray

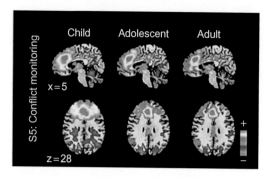

Fig. 2.1. *The cortical connections over childhood (8–12 years) through adolescence (13–17 years), and young adulthood (19–24 years) change from being more diffuse to more focused.* (*Source*: See Ref. 152, reprinted with permission from Oxford University Press.) *(See Plate 10).*

matter. Although the exact relation is not clear, there is general consensus in the literature that synaptic pruning plays a role in these developmental changes.[93,170]

2. With development, we also see dramatic increases in long-range connections between brain regions. With the increase of long-range connections that is dependent on changes in white matter growth and maturation, processing becomes more integrative, involving multiple brain regions (see Figure 2.2). More efficient solutions to processing demands develop. These more efficient network solutions are utilized more frequently and thus increase in connection strength, whereas less efficient connections that are used infrequently decrease in connection strength.

As networks develop, the workload of cognitive processing becomes more widely distributed, spanning multiple brain regions. A benefit to distributing the workload over multiple regions is that the more mature individual has more specialized functional resources to draw upon when performing a task, likely resulting in new and different strategies for problem solving. In addition, the demands on any specific region reduces to some degree. These "freed up" resources can then be allotted to other processing requirements, allowing for greater flexibility in meeting additional environmental demands. For example, as circuitry matures, tasks designed to engage prefrontal activity would require less effort from the prefrontal cortex freeing up its resources for other activities. Over adolescence and into young adulthood, maturational changes are most dramatic for prefrontal networks, which allow for more efficient "top-down" executive control over more "bottom-up" reactive processing.[43,91,140]

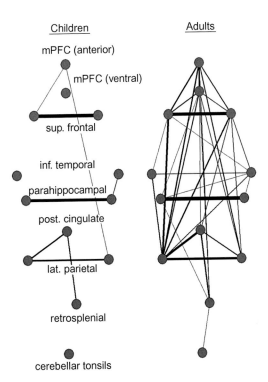

Fig. 2.2. From childhood (7–9 years) to adulthood (21–31 years), we see dramatic increases in long-range connections between regions. (Source: Reprinted with permission from Fair et al., 2008. Copyright (2008) National Academy of Sciences, USA.) (See Plate 11).

Our more refined understanding of network maturation has implications for understanding adolescent behavior. When the frontal networks are not fully mature, there is a greater chance adolescents will need to maximize prefrontal resources during tasks that engage prefrontal activity (i.e., organizing, strategizing, planning, or regulating emotion). Additional stressors in the environment, whether unexpected or ongoing (family, social, or illness-related), can lead to impaired behavior and choices for individuals who are already working at maximum prefrontal capacity. We must also keep in mind that a sleep-deprived adolescent starts the day with a reduction in prefrontal "load" capacity, and thus the likelihood for "overload" is increased over baseline.

2.2 HOW ARE CHANGES IN CONNECTIVITY RELATED TO DEVELOPMENT IN THE COGNITIVE DOMAIN?

The mental processes involved in cognitive control (i.e., the ability to execute, guide, and monitor desired behaviors) steadily improve throughout

BOX 2.1   Can We Measure Brain Age?

One particular network is of special interest. This network—usually called the Default Mode Network or sometimes the Resting State Network—links central brain regions that consistently monitor our internal mental state when we are not dealing with externally presented challenges.[214] It is now becoming apparent that this picture of brain activity—keeping in mind that the brain is never inactive, even in sleep—may hold clues to major developmental brain anomalies, including those in psychopathology (autism, schizophrenia, attention deficit hyperactivity disorder (ADHD), depression, and so on). The development of the Default Mode Network has now been clearly documented as slow and long, stretching from childhood to adulthood.[92]

Given the dramatic developmental changes in connectivity during the resting state, there is some hope that these measures, which require the person to lie still for only a few minutes, may eventually yield a measure of "brain maturity." There is increasing discussion concerning using this type of measure for forensic issues in the United States.[250,251,254] A recent prominent paper illustrated how well this might be eventually applied.[80] The key to properly linking connectivity to brain age is to differentiate between those circuits that increase and those that decrease in strength over time. When only an overall measure of connectivity is taken into account, the overlap from 7 to 30 years is great, despite the obvious general increase. However, when the complexity of the connectivity is taken into account, with some circuits increasing and some decreasing with age, a fairly useful formula separating those under versus those over 18 years of age emerges, with accuracy at over 90% in three large cohorts.[80] This formula makes use of six main connecting systems, but it is interesting that the strongest factor involves networks within the prefrontal cortex. Although much more normative data collection will be needed, especially across various demographic groups, before the data will be accepted as forensic evidence, the differences are apparently great enough to serve as a general indicator of maturation in the same way computerized axial tomography (CAT) scans have been used to indicate normal aging or psychopathology.

childhood, adolescence, and into young adulthood.[35,45,71,171,221] A review of brain development over this period shows that core networks necessary for cognitive control are present in childhood, but the ability to consistently and flexibly recruit these networks increases with age (particularly for the networks connecting frontal regions with parietal and with the striatal regions of the basal ganglia).[169,170] The increased efficiency and specialization of frontal lobe areas is evident across a variety of tasks and research methods. The shifting of the balance towards more frontal lobe control (through its increased connectivity to other brain areas) is considered to be the biological basis for the maturation of behavior. For example, the development of effective self-regulation—the ability to delay gratification of immediate reward in order to follow the rules, make choices, and maintain goals—depends heavily on the development of the networks involved in cognitive control.

When we examine changes in the cognitive domain with age, the implications for the healthy development of frontal networks supporting these functions becomes clear. For example, an important ability that facilitates problem solving, decision making, and the voluntary control of behavior is the capacity to keep relevant information available and "online," a capacity referred to as *working memory*.[10] Working memory involves the ability to maintain, attend to, update, and evaluate information. Although the ability to use working memory is in place in childhood, the more voluntary, flexible, and consistent use of working memory increases over adolescence and adulthood. There are several brain regions known to support working memory, including parietal and frontal regions. Parietal regions support the ability to maintain information for "online" processing, whereas frontal regions allow for the conscious evaluation and manipulation of this information.[64,169,262] The cognitive and behavioral changes associated with working memory over development have been related to the maturation of networks, particularly the connections between frontal and parietal regions.[169,170]

We can see a similar pattern with other cognitive processes that aid in decision making, planning, and voluntary control of behavior. For example, behavioral studies using gambling tasks show that adolescents are more likely to take risks than adults.[33,271] Imaging studies have shown that a particular region of the prefrontal cortex (the ventromedial prefrontal cortex) is associated with the capacity to evaluate risk and reward to guide decision making.[66] We know from our previous discussion that this is one of the last regions to mature. Thus, as connections to this region increase and strengthen (i.e., frontostriatal networks), adolescents can more effectively recruit regions of the brain that are best equipped to compare risk versus reward.

Similarly, the maturation of frontal networks (e.g., frontostriatal and frontoparietal) over adolescence increases the capacity for logical thinking, control of impulses, and performance efficiency.[56,65,262] It is important to keep in mind that all of these processes interact to produce self-regulated adaptive behavior. For example, studies show that young people with greater capacity for working memory are also able to more readily delay immediate gratification in the service of achieving a future goal.[232]

2.3 IMPLICATIONS

Although we have known for quite some time that biological and environmental factors (including enrichment or adversity) can influence brain development, we thought that such influences were most important during the early years between birth and the age of 3 years. We have come to realize that the period from late childhood (onset of puberty) to early adulthood is also an extraordinarily important time for brain development. It is a time of dramatic brain changes, including a surge of synaptogenesis around the onset of puberty that is followed by experience-dependent pruning and myelination of white matter. The important changes that are occurring into young adulthood will ultimately determine the healthy or unhealthy establishment of frontal networks, the networks that support higher order cognitive functions and behavioral regulation.

Here we have focused on general maturational trends; however, we know that there are individual differences in the development and strength of these networks. As we will discuss, variation across individuals in network strength may be related to differences in self-regulation, possibly contributing to risk-taking behavior and anxiety. An important implication for our developing youth stems from the general consensus among researchers that changes in network development and connection strength are dependent on experience. This implies that the wiring of important brain circuitry, particularly the wiring of circuits involved in cognitive control and self-regulation, is vulnerable to experience over the adolescent period. Whether the developing child/adolescent spends considerable time engaging in sports, video games, negotiating family stress, or taking illicit drugs matters and may have long-lasting effects on how their brain is wired.

CHAPTER 3

Social and Emotional Development

Adolescence is a time in life for forging new territory and forming new relationships. It is a time when preteens transition from being dependent on caregivers to becoming independent young adults, which includes a shift from more family-oriented to more peer-oriented interactions. It is well known that this developmental period is characterized by increases in the appeal of novelty and excitement and in the desire to explore and take risks. Similar changes in behavior accompany the onset of puberty across mammalian species and have been shown to have adaptive value, including helping to facilitate emigration away from the home territory and the avoidance of inbreeding that may result in less viable offspring. Although human adolescent novelty-seeking and risk-taking behavior is not typically regarded in a positive light, the positive implications of these behaviors are well known. For example, increased time spent with peers can lead to new social skills and increased social support. Similarly, increased desire for novelty, excitement, and risk taking can lead to opportunities to explore adult behavior and privileges and to becoming more adept at negotiating life challenges. Collectively, these changes during adolescence provide the motivation to explore new areas of social life and sexuality outside of the home, which will ultimately lead to a transition from the family home to autonomous living. Unfortunately, many of these changes also come with considerable costs. Adolescence is also a time of increased drug use and unprotected sex, and the three highest causes of mortality in adolescents are accidents, homicides, and suicides.[143]

During the transition from childhood to adolescence, there are also notable changes in emotionality and in self-regulation. There is an increase in the experience of negative emotions and emotions fluctuate more frequently, become more intense, and more subject to extremes than those experienced by children and adults.[239] There are also transitions in behavioral regulation. In childhood, behavioral regulation is more externally derived from the guidance and constraints put in place by parents and caregivers, whereas in adolescence, there is an increasing need for self-regulation. The way in which changes in emotionality and self-regulation are negotiated will greatly influence how well the adolescent navigates through his or her expanding social world. How effectively pre-teens and adolescents learn to self-regulate impulses and emotions will influence not only decisions about participation in dangerous activities, but also vulnerability to psychopathology. This is especially important considering that the lifetime risk for the emergence of psychopathology peaks at age 14.[153]

In this section, we will discuss brain changes related to social and emotional development over childhood, adolescence, and young adult-hood. We will conclude the chapter with a consideration of individual differences in brain-based aspects of personality and the influence such differences may have for risk and resilience to psychopathology.

3.1 THE DEVELOPMENT OF SOCIAL INFORMATION PROCESSING

Humans are an immensely social species. We create friendships, love relationships, family units, social groups, societies, and cultures. In the service of social communication, our brains have developed spe-cialized networks to receive and process social information. These net-works allow us to recognize others, to be aware of their perspectives, and to evaluate their desires, beliefs, and intentions. A simple model of social information processing has been put forth by Nelson and col-leagues.[190] This model distinguishes three basic networks or systems that are involved in the processing of social information:

1. The *detection node* is responsible for the detection and categorization of social objects or events that we sense in our environment (social stimuli).
2. The *affective node* attaches emotional significance to social stimuli, such as whether the social stimulus is rewarding or punishing.
3. The *cognitive-regulatory node* includes complex cognitive processes, such as perceiving and interpreting the mental states of others, the regulation of impulses, and the generation of goal-directed behaviors.

The areas of the brain associated with each node are shown in Figure 3.1. Changes occur in each of these systems over development. Although for simplicity social information processing is divided into three basic compo-nents, it should be understood that the processing of social information involves reciprocal relations among each of these systems.

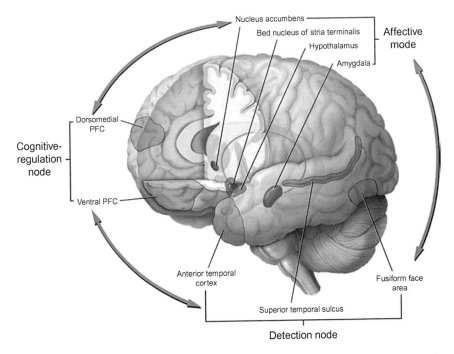

Fig. 3.1. Brain regions that make up the detection node (highlighted in green) are responsible for carrying out the basic perceptual processes of social stimuli. Brain regions that make up the affective node (highlighted in red) interact with the detection node to attach emotional significance to the stimuli. Brain regions that make up the cognitive-regulatory node (highlighted in blue) are involved in controlling response tendencies and understanding others' perspectives. (Source: Reproduced with permission from Ref. 190.) (See Plate 12).

3.1.1 The Detection of Social Signals: Face Perception

The ability to quickly and accurately perceive socially relevant stimuli in the environment has the potential to provide a wealth of cues such as threats, warnings, and rewards that help to guide adaptive behavior. The most common and well-studied social stimulus that we perceive is the human face. Facial expressions are a rich source of social signals conveying focus of attention, intention, motivation, and emotion to the observer. Faces are so important for social communication in our species that specialized brain networks have evolved for their perception! Indeed, within a few hours of birth newborns appear to show an innate preference to attend to face-like objects.[94]

Brain imaging studies have shown that the perception of faces involves the coordinated activity of several cortical and subcortical regions, most notably the *fusiform face area* (FFA), a region on the underside of the temporal lobe.[129] Developmental research has shown that the maturation of these specialized "face" networks is not complete until adulthood. Indeed, the size of the area of FFA activity increases from late childhood (7–11 years) to adolescence (12–16 years) and into adulthood (18–35 years), with the area of adult FFA activation being three times that of a child's.[116] Other studies have found similar developmental patterns[224] including the continued refinement of connections within the face perception networks into adulthood.[63]

3.1.2 Learning and Reacting to Emotional Information

The information that we perceive in our social world is paired with some level of emotional significance. The affective network reacts to this emotional content. For example, certain stimuli are associated with reward, making them more approachable, whereas others have aversive qualities such as punishment or pain, making them ones to avoid. The amygdala is a particularly prominent player in this network and is involved with learning the emotional significance of stimuli that we encounter in our environment, for example associating them with either pleasure or pain. There are numerous neural connections that converge onto the amygdala from other brain regions to communicate information. The amygdala also contains numerous receptors for hormones, which allow circulating hormones to trigger its activity. For example, when *cortisol*, the body's stress hormone, attaches to its receptors, the amygdala is activated and propagates the stress-related response to other brain regions.

The amygdala communicates with the stress system through its connections to the hypothalamus and to other brain regions involved in the regulation of arousal. In this way, the emotional significance that it has attached to a stimulus can influence arousal and help to organize a rapid behavioral response (e.g., flight or fight when sensing danger).

During adolescence, there are notable changes in amygdala volume (see Chapter 1). Studies with animals have shown that neuronal connections that activate certain regions of the amygdala also undergo significant changes over the adolescent period.[69] Accompanying these changes is a marked increase in the activity of the *hypothalamic pituitary adrenal (HPA) axis*, the body's stress system, which results in a marked increase in cortisol.[277] Changes in these systems make adolescence an extremely vulnerable time for the interactions of stress and emotional arousal (see section 3.3.1).

Several studies have reported that the ability to accurately identify emotional faces continues to increase from childhood and into adolescence, although the developmental trajectory of these abilities seems to differ somewhat according to the emotion.[37] For example, some research shows that the accurate identification of fear increases linearly across childhood and adolescence until it reaches adult levels, whereas the ability to accurately identify anger remains relatively stable at an immature level and then increases dramatically between adolescence and adulthood.

Importantly, there are also individual differences in the ability to accurately identify emotional faces. Children who have experienced a history of abuse more readily misinterpret ambiguous faces as angry and also show increased brain responses to angry faces compared with children who have not experienced abuse.[208–211] This line of investigation suggests that individual differences in learning play a key role in the detection and response to emotional faces.

Several studies have shown that the activation of the brain's emotional systems during emotional face perception, particularly the perception of fearful faces, is greater for adolescents compared with children and adults,[123,127,184] although this finding is not consistent.[37] The inconsistency across studies may be due in part to individual differences in emotional responding to faces. For example, the initial reactivity to an emotional stimulus, such as a fearful face, is stronger than the response to repeated presentations. The magnitude of the initial emotional response typically decreases rapidly with repeated presentations of a stimulus, an effect known as *habituation*. However, there are individual differences in habituation. Some individuals do not show the typical reduction or "recovery" from an initial emotional response; that is, they are slower to habituate. Most studies that have examined the emotional response to faces have used the average of all responses, which in some cases, depending on the variability, may wash out the effects.

Findings from a recent study highlight the importance of individual differences.[127] In this study, brain responses to fearful, happy, and neutral faces were measured in children, adolescents, and adults. The researchers found that overall activity in the amygdala regions for fearful faces was greater for adolescents than for children or adults. This finding indicates that, on average, adolescents show greater emotional responsiveness to fearful faces (see Figure 3.2). When examining this

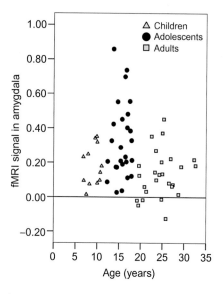

Fig. 3.2. *Amygdala functional magnetic resonance imaging (fMRI) responses across age. As can be seen, adolescents show not only larger average responses but also greater variation in responses.* (*Source:* See Ref. 127.)

graph and comparing across groups, it is clear that there is increased variability in amygdala activation during the adolescent period rather than simply an increase in the overall activity. Many adolescents respond with amygdala activation in the same range as that of children and adults, but many others respond with greater activation. This variability could be due to many factors, including individual differences in the ability to effectively self-regulate emotional response.

In order to obtain an approximate measure of individual differences in regulatory control, researchers examined the habituation of amygdala activity to consecutive presentations of fearful faces. A reduction in amygdala activity with repeated presentations is thought to reflect emotional regulation, which would be mediated by connections from frontal "control" regions to amygdala regions. In other words, increased activity in frontal regions should be related to the degree of reductions in subcortical amygdala activity. Indeed, these researchers found that the strength of the relationship between frontal areas and amygdala activity (measured by the inverse relationship of their activity) predicted the degree to which amygdala activity reduced after repeated exposure to fearful faces. This finding suggests that the ability to reduce one's response to emotionally arousing faces depends on the strength of the connections between frontal and amygdala regions. Interestingly, this study also collected measures of how anxious a person tends to be in everyday life (called trait anxiety). Individuals who reported higher levels of trait anxiety showed less habituation in amygdala activity with repeated exposure to fearful faces. This finding suggests that individuals who tend to exhibit high trait anxious behavior (i.e., feel anxiety in their daily life) may not be able to control their reactions to social stimuli as well as those who are low on this measure.

Findings such as those described above emphasize the importance of individual differences in the strength of connections between frontal and subcortical regions and their consequent effects on emotional regulation. Strength in connectivity may be influenced by multiple genetic and environmental factors. Following this line of investigation, several animal studies have identified candidate genes (and genetic variants) that may be implicated in reduced habituation (an indicator of reduced emotional regulation) to fear-related cues in the environment.[238]

3.1.2.1 Implications
As we know from Chapters 1 and 2, differences in connections are not hardwired and immutable. We can, therefore, consider how experience may play a role. Individuals who are unable to effectively regulate emotion are at risk for psychopathologies, such as anxiety and depression. This risk is elevated during early adolescence, a time when frontal regions are not fully mature. Learning effective emotion-regulation techniques may facilitate the strengthening of these pathways. The enhancement of such skills may not only reduce risk and severity but may also prevent the onset of disorder.

3.1.3 Complex Cognitive Processes Involved in Processing Social Information
Thus far, we have discussed the processing of social information with respect to perception and emotional reactivity. When we add the higher-order cognitive functions of the frontal cortex to this mix, we can begin to examine mental functions that influence social cognition, such as perceiving and interpreting the mental state of others, empathic understanding, and sensitivity to social acceptance and rejection.

Indeed, research involving patients with frontal lobe damage show how important the frontal regions are for social cognition. Patients with damage to these regions show deficits in functions such as social awareness, social decision making, and the generation of abstract knowledge related to social and moral expectations.[190]

3.1.4 Theory of Mind

A critical component of social information processing that involves higher-order cognitive processing is the ability to infer the mental states of others. As we communicate with others, we are readily able to read their social/emotional responses and to understand what they are thinking or feeling as well as their intentions. The ability to attribute mental states (thoughts, wishes, feelings, or beliefs) is referred to as *theory of mind* or *mentalizing* in the social neuroscience literature. The brain regions that make up the theory of mind network have been identified. The regions include the temporoparietal junction, the area where the temporal and parietal lobes meet, which is involved in distinguishing self from others, and the medial prefrontal cortex, which is involved in regulatory control.

The development of theory of mind in the first year after birth has been the focus of a considerable amount of behavioral research. The development of cognitive abilities that provide the foundation for theory of mind include the ability to understand intentions, to differentiate between belief and reality, and to understand that others can have beliefs about the world that are different from one's own. These foundational abilities are seen in children at about 4–5 years of age.[30]

Recent studies have used a variety of tasks to investigate the continued development of theory of mind over childhood, adolescence, and adulthood.[37] Cross-sectional studies involving children, adolescents, and adults consistently show a decrease in the activity of medial prefrontal cortex from childhood to adulthood when individuals engage in mentalizing tasks. A recent study demonstrated that adolescents show stronger activity between regions of the theory of mind network, including the medial prefrontal cortex, compared with adults, possibly indicating greater effort required in these tasks and less efficiency.

In line with this, behavioral performance on a rule-based nonmentalizing task (relying solely on executive control) was shown to remain the same between late adolescence and adulthood, while significant improvements occurred with respect to accuracy on a mentalizing task.[83] These findings suggest that the ability to effectively use theory of mind (including the effective evaluation of another person's perspective) continues to develop into adulthood. Collectively, the above findings indicate that the late maturation of prefrontal regions likely influences the maturation of mentalizing functions. Similar to the developmental trends in other domains, abilities for basic theory of mind abilities are in place in early childhood, but there is a gradual shift in the efficient use of frontal networks when performing these tasks as the child matures. These changes are especially important between adolescence and adulthood when frontal maturation is elaborated.

3.1.5 Empathy

Overlapping in some respects with the process of theory of mind is another important process for effective social communication, the ability to feel empathy for others. Empathy has been defined as "an affective response that stems from the apprehension or comprehension of another's emotional state or condition and is similar to what the other person is feeling or would be expected to feel" (p. 671).[85] The ability to empathize has been related to prosocial behavior, reduced aggression, and is thought to form the basis for moral reasoning.[76,77] Indeed, deficits in empathy are part of the characteristic profile of antisocial personality disorder (previously known as psychopathy), a diagnosis that is prevalent among individuals who do not conform to societal rules, such as violent criminal offenders (as well as a subset of conduct disordered adolescents who may be on the trajectory for such behavior).

Models of the empathic experience include several components:

1. *Emotional arousal*, which involves the rapid processing of emotional information and is related to brain activation in subcortical regions, such as the amygdala and the hypothalamus, and in frontal regions, such as the orbital prefrontal cortex (OFC) (see Figure 3.3).
2. *Emotional understanding*, which involves the awareness of self and others and activates frontal and parietal/temporal regions.
3. *Emotional regulation*, which involves executive functions and connections between subcortical regions of the brain involved in the processing of emotion and frontal regions involved in regulatory control.

The first two components seem to develop fairly early. By 18 months, children display spontaneous helping behaviors as they begin to develop the awareness of self and others. Behavioral research demonstrates that over childhood, the emotional components of empathy emerge earlier than the cognitive components. Other studies have investigated changes in empathy from adolescence to adulthood, including the attainment of mature empathic understanding. Findings suggest that there is a shift in empathy over this period. With maturity, empathy becomes less emotional and more evaluative. Mature empathic understanding or "cognitive

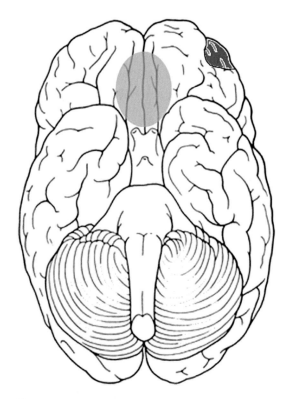

Fig. 3.3. The areas of the frontal cortex active during empathic responses change from the ventromedial portion (in orange) of the orbitofrontal cortex (OFC) in childhood to the lateral OFC (colored blue) in adulthood, with a gradual shift from 10 to 40 years. (Source: See Ref. 77 for original data.) (See Plate 13).

empathy" is thought to include perspective taking and to involve similar brain regions as those involved in theory of mind. The changes in brain activity during empathic response from adolescence to adulthood seem to parallel the behavioral findings. Brain activity shifts from regions of the brain involved in emotional regulation (medial regions of the OFC) to regions involved in executive functioning (lateral regions of the OFC)[76,77] (see Figure 3.3). Findings also suggest that amygdala activity during empathic responding decreases with age, with the implication that emotional responding becomes increasingly controlled with age.

3.1.6 Social Acceptance and Social Rejection

Another issue that ties into the awareness of self and others is the sensitivity to social evaluation, including social acceptance and rejection. Social rejection can occur in many contexts: rejection by an individual, in the context of a friendship or in the context of a romantic relationship (in teenagers and adults) or by groups in the context of bullying or teasing. In childhood, when social rejection is consistent or prolonged, it can lead to loneliness, low self-esteem, internalizing disorder (e.g., depression), and externalizing disorder (e.g., aggression).[180] Once peer rejection is established, it tends to remain stable over time.[61] Several studies have found that adolescent self-reports of sensitivity to peer acceptance and rejection are higher than those of both children and adults. In adolescents aged 13–17 years, peer evaluations were more important than in other age groups for determining self-worth.[229] These differences are not surprising considering that adolescents are transitioning from more family-oriented to more peer-oriented interactions.

Research studies have used a modified version of an internet game to measure how the brain responds to social evaluation. The game, which is called Cyberball, involves three players passing a ball to each other, for which the actions of those other than the participant are pre-programmed. It is designed such that the participant can be included (social inclusion) or excluded (social exclusion) from play at various times throughout the game. In general, findings suggest that social exclusion activates similar brain regions to those activated during the experience of physical pain.[86] Evaluations of changes over development in a group of adolescents (14–16 years) and adults (23–38 years)[230] have shown that adolescents report more distress during the social exclusion period than do adults and that there are also important differences in how their brains responded to this condition. During social exclusion compared with social inclusion, adolescents showed decreased activity in regions of the prefrontal cortex. Adults showed the reverse pattern, a pattern that has also been reported in other studies with adults.[229] The specific regions of the prefrontal cortex that showed reduced activity during social exclusion versus inclusion were the lateral OFC regions. These regions typically show greater activation when people are trying to control their behavior, including their negative feelings. The findings from these studies suggest that, on average, when adolescents are experiencing distress during social exclusion, they may not have the mature frontal activation needed to effectively control these feelings.

We know that social rejection tends to remain stable over time and can lead to isolation and loneliness. In studies with adults, loneliness has been related to poor outcomes such as impaired self-regulation, hostility, negative emotion, and poor health.[39] A recent brain imaging study has examined loneliness and brain response to pictures of pleasant and unpleasant social scenes. Researchers found that people who are not lonely show much greater activity in the ventral striatum (the reward region) when viewing pictures of people enjoying themselves in pleasant settings than do lonely individuals, suggesting that these images are not as rewarding to the lonely individual. Lonely individuals, on the other hand, showed much less activity in the temporoparietal region of the brain (an area involved in perspective taking and distinguishing self from other) when viewing pictures of people in unpleasant settings compared with non-lonely individuals. This may indicate a reduced tendency to "mentalize" or take another's perspective. We cannot know from this study whether the brain differences in response to social stimuli produce loneliness or whether loneliness and social isolation influence brain activity, and of course both may be true, as there may be genetic and psychosocial influences. However, these findings do show that loneliness is related to activity in brain regions that are involved in effective social information processing. Thus, the reported differences in brain function between lonely and non-lonely people may have further implications for differences in social skills between these groups.

Brain-based differences in social information processing may moderate the subjective experience of social rejection and its noted stability across childhood, potentially conferring greater susceptibility to adverse social experiences, such as ostracism and bullying. Although patterns of rejection and social isolation begin early in childhood, adolescence is an important time when sensitivity to peer evaluation increases and is more influential in determining concepts of self-worth. Such factors may increase the risk for behavioral problems and psychopathology.

3.1.7 Implications

Brain imaging studies suggest that the networks involved in social cognition in adolescents have not reached the adult levels of processing efficiency that parallel mature reasoning about what others think and feel or mature levels of empathic understanding. There is also evidence suggesting that adolescents are more sensitive to social evaluations and yet are less able to regulate the emotions surrounding such evaluations compared with adults. These normal developmental changes need to be kept in mind when considering our expectations concerning adolescents' social and emotional responses.

3.2 MODELS OF SOCIAL BEHAVIOR

3.2.1 Current Conceptual Models of Risk-Taking Behavior

Adolescence is a period often associated with impulsivity and thrill-seeking behavior leading to dangerous and sometimes fatal activities. Although it is an exaggeration to attribute these characteristics to all adolescents, there is certainly justification for concern with respect to some. As indicated earlier, research on brain maturation has shown that networks involved in the experience of emotion mature earlier than those involved in the higher order "executive" functions of planning and control. There is general consensus in the field that the imbalance created by this difference in maturation rates can lead to a surge of risk-taking behavior early in adolescence when self-regulation has not fully matured.

To fully understand the current models of increased risk-taking behavior during adolescence, we must first distinguish puberty from adolescence. Puberty, often used to measure the onset of the adolescent period, is the process of sexual maturation that leads to the development of secondary sexual characteristics, sexual interests, and an adult body capable of sexual reproduction. The fluctuations in hormones during this time are thought to be partly responsible for the sex differences in brain growth patterns during adolescence.[109] The brain regions likely affected by the hormonal changes include those involved in learning, memory, and experience of emotion, such as the amygdala and hippocampus.

Pubertal hormone changes may lead to an increased sensitivity to emotion.[43,90,249] Evidence for these changes comes from several lines of research. For example, both men and women with increased testosterone levels (due to endocrine disorders) show greater activity in limbic brain regions when viewing fearful faces than do healthy controls.[91,187] Cross-sectional studies have also examined activity in limbic regions during a variety of tasks across normally developing children, adolescents, and adults.[44,89,101] These studies generally report that adolescents show greater activity in these regions compared with adults and children, particularly in response to the receipt of reward.

In line with these findings, behavior driven by sensation-seeking (the desire for or enjoyment of high-sensation and high-arousal experiences) has been shown to change over development. Sensation seeking is thought to play a major role in adolescent risk-taking behavior, including risky sexual behavior, drug use, and cigarette smoking.[5,6] The brain areas that are involved in the desire for high sensation are the same as those that are involved in the experience of reward. A series of studies by Steinberg and colleagues have shown that the developmental pattern for the sensitivity to rewards,[47] the preference for immediate rewards,[252] and sensation seeking[249] increase in early adolescence, and then decline and remain relatively stable through young adulthood.[47] This pattern resembles an inverted-U shape (see Figure 3.4 and the bottom portion of Figure 3.5). This developmental pattern is thought to be linked to hormonal changes and consequent brain changes occurring over puberty. Indeed, sensation seeking is more strongly related to pubertal changes than to age.[244,248]

Findings from these same studies and others show a different developmental pattern for cognitive control or executive functions. Impulse control,[47,249] anticipation of future consequences,[252] strategic planning,[1,2] and resistance to peer influence[253] follow a linear pattern, increasing with age over the adolescent period (e.g., see the top of Figure 3.5, which shows a linear decrease in impulsivity or equivalently, an increase in impulse control). These executive control functions are more heavily influenced by age and experience and the maturation of frontal regions, which is still

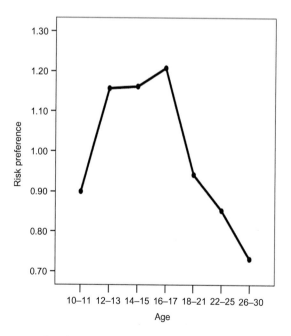

Fig. 3.4. Age differences in risk preference. (Source: See Ref. 250.)

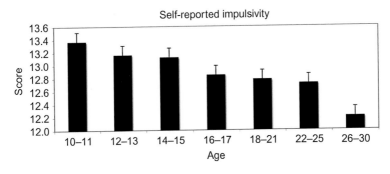

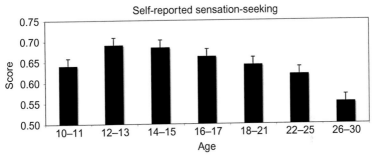

Fig. 3.5. Self-reported impulsivity and sensation seeking for over 900 participants aged from 10 to 30 years demonstrate a distribution dropping to adult levels only at the end of 20 years. (Source: From Ref. 249.)

occurring late in adolescence and into early adulthood. In line with this, brain imaging has shown that activity in the ventral striatum (the primary reward region of the brain, see Box 3.1) in response to monetary reward is related to self-reports of risk-taking behavior, but not to impulsive behavior, which would be influenced by activity in frontal regions.[101]

BOX 3.1 Where Reward is Experienced in the Brain

Nucleus accumbens: This structure is part of the ventral striatum (part of the limbic pathway) and is the dopamine response center for rewards.

Other dopamine-sensitive structures in this network include the amygdala and ventral tegmental area.

The timing of these behavioral changes may have implications for interventions designed to reduce adolescent risk-taking behavior. For example, Steinberg suggests "…that interventions designed to capitalize on adolescents' heightened propensity for reward seeking (e.g., emphasizing the rewarding aspects of alternatives to the risky behavior one wants to prevent) might be especially effective among younger adolescents but less so among older ones, whereas those that capitalize on a growing capacity for self-regulation (e.g., encouraging adolescents to pause and think before engaging in a risky behavior) might be more effective among older teenagers than among younger ones" (p. 745).[250]

Although current models of adolescent risk taking converge on a central theme of the mismatch created by differences in maturation rates for reward seeking and cognitive control, they differ with respect to the emphasis on factors that may influence this relationship. For example, Ernst and colleagues highlight the imbalance between sensitivity to reward and reduced sensitivity to punishment, and the ability of the cognitive control system to regulate this imbalance over development.[89] Steinberg and colleagues[250] focus on the influence of peers on this balance and much of their work substantiates well-known anecdotal evidence of peer pressure.

3.2.2 The Triadic Model of Motivated Behavior in Adolescence

The triadic model suggests that our behavior and emotional states can be best conceptualized as the balance between two very basic motivational systems, the motivation to approach a stimulus that has been associated with reward or pleasure and the motivation to withdraw from a stimulus that has been associated with punishment or pain. These two motivational systems are regulated by cognitive control (see Figure 3.6).

Although the view that our behavior can be mapped onto a two-dimensional space seems rather simplistic, it has its roots in studies of

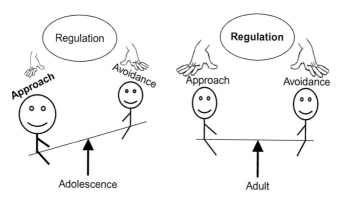

Fig. 3.6. A triadic model of motivated behavior. (Source: See Ref. 89.)

animal behavior, which show the conservation of these basic systems in all species ranging from insects to mammals. We learn and organize our behavior and make decisions about how to behave according to two basic principles: we approach stimuli that are rewarding and we withdraw from those that are punishing, harmful, or threatening. Several models propose that all emotions, and human behavior more generally, are organized around these two primary systems.[42,72,157]

The neural networks that underlie these motivational systems have been extensively studied in animals and humans. The primary region involved in the approach motivation network is part of the ventral striatum region of the basal ganglia. The primary region involved in withdrawal-related motivation is the amygdala. Cognitive/regulatory control of these systems is supported through connections between these regions and the prefrontal cortex, more specifically the ventromedial regions of the prefrontal cortex (see Figure 1.3).

We know that these basic systems are interconnected. The likelihood of a person engaging in a risky behavior is based not only on their anticipation of reward but also on the possibility of punishment. Cognitive/regulatory control helps to evaluate and regulate these feelings. Ernst and colleagues propose that, during adolescence, the balance between approach- and avoidance-motivated behavior is tilted toward approach, during a time when cognitive control is not fully mature. This model has found some support. Several studies have shown that activity in the reward system upon the receipt of reward is greater during adolescence compared with adulthood.[91,102] For example, a study that examined brain reward system activity in response to reward across three age groups—children (7–11 years), adolescents (13–17 years), and adults (23–29 years)—found that activity increased over all age groups with increasing reward value. However, adolescents showed much greater activity in these regions than both children and adults.[102] There is also evidence that the amygdala in adolescents is less active in response to feedback indicating loss, suggesting that not only are adolescents more prone to be stimulated by reward but that they may also be less reactive to indicators of punishment.[89,91] We must also keep in mind that there are individual differences in the response to reward and the understanding of consequences. A follow-up study showed that the degree of activity in reward regions was related to the likelihood that an individual would participate in a risky behavior and to the expectation that this behavior would result in a positive outcome.[101]

3.2.3 Activity in Reward Regions and Interactions With Cognitive Control

The idea proposed by Ernst and others is that reward activity increases during a time when cognitive control has not fully matured. In this context, there is a greater push for reward based on the increased sensitivity to the rewarding qualities of a risky action during a period when there are fewer cognitive resources to draw upon. Several studies have investigated the relationship between activity in the reward system and the ability to control behavior.[207] A few studies have also considered these relationships across development.[104,144,239]

The relationship between reward system activity and cognitive control seems to depend on the type of task used. For example, a recent study examined participants' ability to inhibit a behavioral response to either positive (rewarding) or neutral face expressions.[239] The task required participants to press a button if the presented face was different from the previously presented face. However, if the same face repeated, the participant's job was to withhold responding. In this study, errors (responding when the response should have been withheld) reduced with age, as would be expected, but only for the neutral condition. The errors to happy faces followed an inverted-U pattern. The errors were greater for adolescents than for children or adults. The activity in the ventral striatum was also much greater in adolescents than other age groups in response to happy faces. This study suggests that, under certain conditions, increased activation in reward regions during adolescence may interfere with task performance.

In other experiments, the rewarding stimulus is presented as an incentive to perform better on the task. When rewards are used as incentives, task performance improves. This effect has been shown to be greater for adolescents than adults.[104,126,144] Interestingly, in general, studies show that money, a nonsocial reward, is a better reinforcer for performance than social rewards. Again, we must keep in mind that there are individual differences. A recent finding has indicated that personality traits may determine the extent to which types of rewards influence performance.[155] For example, those children (aged 8–12 years) who were rated by parents as being higher on risk taking showed larger improvements on cognitive control performance when money, a nonsocial reward, was used to reinforce behavior. On the other hand, there was a tendency for children rated higher in empathy to benefit more from social rewards, such as happy and exuberant faces.

3.2.4 Hot and Cold Cognition

In general, findings concerning decision making suggest that younger adolescents are more influenced by immediate rewards than future rewards.[1,2] The ability to make good decisions at any age, however, depends on many factors, including the ability to stay focused and to avoid distractions, which improves with maturity. Emotions may also influence decision making as they can be a distraction that interferes with cognitive control. In the last decade, there has been a surge of interest in the distinction between "hot" (emotionally charged) and "cold" (deliberate and analytical) decision making.[70]

A study comparing adolescents (13–16 years) and adults (20–38 years) on "hot" and "cold" decision making provides important insight into risk-taking behavior in adolescents.[97] Adolescents seem to be able to evaluate information and make decisions similar to adults when emotions are not involved, during "cold" or deliberate decision making. However, when emotions played a role, during "hot" decision making, adolescents made riskier decisions and used less information to make those decisions compared with adults.

3.2.5 Peer Influence Model

Adolescents may often find themselves in decision-making situations when they are feeling emotionally charged, such as when they are being emotionally influenced by peers to engage in risky acts. It has been shown many times that adolescents are not generally tempted to partake in risky behaviors,[218] but the presence of peers is a key influence. There are forensic implications for peer influence,[251] including driving dangerously,[236] abusing drugs,[16] and committing criminal activities.[283]

According to one model of risk-taking behavior, the presence of peers increases the activity of the reward system, so that socially induced behaviors, including those involving risks, become more rewarding to the adolescent. For example, adolescents (13–16 years) are much more likely to play video games in a risky manner when they are in the company of peers than are young adults in their early twenties or older adults.[103] Steinberg's lab has shown that merely knowing that friends are watching their performance on external monitors alters adolescents' activation of the brain's reward system during a video game in which points are gained by taking risks.[52] This study also showed that when peers were present, the activity in the reward system increased,

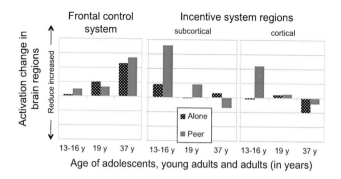

Fig. 3.7. Increases in brain activation as a function of playing a driver simulation video game alone and with peers. The frontal control system (dorsolateral prefrontal cortex) does not differentiate conditions. The subcortical incentive system (ventral striatum) and the cortical incentive system (orbitofrontal cortex) show greater increase in activation for adolescents when with peers than for older participants. (Source: Data from Ref. 52.)

although the frontal control regions did not show any differences in activity between peer and alone conditions (see Figure 3.7).

Similar research has examined the response of cortical regions specifically during the presentation of negative feedback during a risk-taking video game, where the participant loses points by crashing his car in a game of "chicken." The game was played alone and also with two friends present, whose job was to encourage and comment on the participant's performance.[231] By recording the electroencephalogram (EEG; electrical brain signals from the scalp) during each condition, it was shown that when peers were present, frontal lobe activity (in the medial prefrontal region) in response to the negative feedback was reduced compared with when participants were alone. However, there were large individual differences in this response. For example, participants who were more prone to surgency (the tendency to be active, to experience positive emotion, and to enjoy seeking excitement) showed a greater reduction in frontal activity when peers were present, compared with those low on this measure. The lower frontal activity to negative feedback for those prone to surgency may reflect a tendency to be less influenced by punishment cues, whereas those lower on these measures who show greater activity in frontal regions may be more careful and watchful when among peers.

Of course, these differences may also relate to the ability to effectively regulate the arousal. Brain connectivity was examined while 10-year-old boys and girls watched emotionally charged video clips. Children who were better able to resist the influence of peers during social interactions showed greater connectivity within frontal regions and between frontal and parietal regions.[119] Together, these studies suggest that the presence of peers activates reward regions of the brain and influences risk-taking behavior. However, the degree to which individuals are susceptible to this influence may depend on individual differences in reactivity and in frontal lobe control.

3.3 AGGRESSION

Brain-based models of aggression focus on the amygdala, the ventromedial prefrontal cortex (see Figures 1.3 and 1.9), and the connections between these two regions. Two subtypes of aggression have received considerable attention—reactive and proactive (or instrumental). Reactive aggression is "hot" or emotional aggression that occurs in response to a specific provocation or to frustration. The individual reacts aggressively without a specific goal in mind. Proactive or instrumental aggression is "cold" or deliberate, goal-oriented aggression and need not be accompanied by an emotional state. Furthermore, these subtypes are specific with respect to risk for psychopathology. Reactive aggression is associated with diagnoses of conduct disorder, post-traumatic stress disorder, bipolar disorder, and intermittent explosive disorder, whereas instrumental aggression is associated with diagnoses of antisocial personality disorder (psychopathy).

The neurobiological basis for these subtypes is also thought to differ. Reactive aggression is a behavior that is displayed in all mammals and has been extensively studied. This "reactive circuitry" includes subcortical brain regions (i.e., the amygdala, hypothalamus and periaqueductal gray region of the midbrain) that are regulated by regions of the prefrontal cortex. Reactive aggression is thought to involve hypersensitivity of this circuitry paired with reduced frontal control, likely due to reduced connectivity between these regions. Support for this model comes from several sources.[67] For example, differences in amygdala volume in adolescents aged 11–13 years have been related to aggression during parental interactions,[279] possibly reflecting increased vulnerability to emotional states. In a functional activation study of males aged 14–17, the tendency to be angry was related to lower activity in ventromedial prefrontal regions during imagined aggressive behavior compared with imagined nonaggressive behavior.[256] The ventromedial prefrontal cortex has connections with brain regions involved in emotion processing, such as the amygdala. Thus, trait anger may reflect a reduction in the regulation of impulses by prefrontal regions.

In the case of instrumental aggression, individuals use aggression as a means to obtain a goal. The neural systems underlying this type of aggression are also involved in learning reinforcement value and evaluating behavioral options. The ability to learn that certain social stimuli represent threat, pain or punishment, or reward is crucial for understanding social reinforcement, and the difference between what is morally correct or incorrect. For example, early in normal development, children learn that certain behaviors associated with fearful and sad faces are to be avoided.

As we have previously discussed, the amygdala is important for learning or instilling stimuli with emotional qualities that will help guide future behavior. When these associations are made, this information is projected to frontal regions for evaluation (i.e., to the medial regions of the prefrontal cortex). In this way, the frontal cortex can compare and evaluate the options. Instrumental aggression is thought to involve impairments in the learning functions of the amygdala, the evaluative functions of the prefrontal areas, and the functional connections between these regions.

This model has received support from studies of adults with psychopathy. Psychopathy is characterized by an abnormal lack of empathy and amoral conduct, including a tendency to manipulate and violate the boundaries of others. Studies of adults with psychopathic traits show that individuals high on these measures show under-activation of amygdala regions and alterations of prefrontal regions during the processing of emotions compared with healthy controls. The earliest study to examine brain mechanisms with respect to psychopathic traits in children was in 2008. Findings from this study suggest that adolescents with psychopathic tendencies also show reduced amygdala activity to fearful faces and a reduction in functional connectivity between the amygdala and prefrontal regions during the processing of emotional faces.[67] Developmental research in this area is just beginning and there is still much to be done to understand brain-based mechanisms that may influence the trajectory of psychopathy and genetic and environmental factors that may increase risk.

3.3.1 Violence

Violence is typically regarded as a subset of aggressive behavior. A number of psychological traits and environmental factors have been associated with the emergence of violent behavior in youth[162] (see Box 3.2).

> **BOX 3.2 Factors involved in the emergence of violent behavior in youth**
>
> Psychological traits
>   sensation seeking
>   hyperactivity
>   problems with concentration
> Environmental factors
>   extreme poverty
>   family adversity
>   delinquent peers

Puberty may also play a role. In a large study with about 3000 participants, the stage of pubertal development was related to violent behavior in children aged 10–15 years. Regardless of age, children in mid and late stages of puberty exhibited a three-fold increase of violence compared with children in the early stage of puberty.[131]

Developmental brain changes associated with age and puberty may lead to some individuals being more susceptible to risk factors, such as sensation seeking, involvement with delinquent peers, and sensitivity to environmental stress.

3.4 INDIVIDUAL DIFFERENCES IN SOCIAL BEHAVIOR: A PERSONALITY PERSPECTIVE

We are well aware that people differ with respect to their personality traits. Some people are sociable and exuberant—full of positive emotions. Others are shy, constrained in their behavior, and may focus more on negative qualities of people and situations. There is a considerable amount of research that has focused on aspects of personality that may be more biologically than environmentally influenced. The word "temperament" is used to describe more biologically influenced aspects of personality.[38] Temperament has been defined as biologically based differences in reactivity and self-regulation, influenced over time by heredity, maturation, and experience.[219] Individual differences in temperament are considered stable and enduring tendencies to react with a characteristic style and intensity to life experiences and are believed to be predictive of psychopathology.[219] Inherent in this definition is the notion that some temperamental styles may be more vulnerable than others to different emotional states, possibly conferring greater risk.

Stable differences in temperament are paralleled by individual differences in the activity of brain networks, including the motivational/emotional networks, such as the approach and avoidance motivational systems. Jeffrey Gray's model of personality proposes that differences in the sensitivity of these brain-based motivational systems, whether genetically or environmentally induced, form the basis of our differences in personality and behavior.[118] It distinguishes two neural motivational systems that regulate sensitivity to punishment and reward. The Behavioral Inhibition System (BIS) is based on the avoidance motivational system and is related to more introverted and anxious personality styles. The Behavioral Activation System (BAS) is based on the approach motivation system and is related to more extroverted and sensation-seeking personality styles. Accumulating evidence from adult studies suggest that an imbalance in BIS and BAS may influence risk for certain forms of psychopathology. For example, hyperactivity of the BIS has been related to anxiety disorders, whereas hyperactivity in the BAS has been related to substance abuse and aggressive/disruptive disorders.

The tendency to experience more positive or more negative emotion is also based on these motivational systems. More avoidance-oriented personality styles, such as shy and introverted types, are reported to experience more negative emotion (such as fearfulness, sadness, and disgust), whereas more approach-oriented types have a tendency to experience more positive emotions (such as happiness and joy). Either predisposition in the extreme can confer risk for psychopathology.[225] When frontal regions are not fully mature, a predisposition to experience extreme exuberance without effective regulation may lead to more thrill-seeking and reckless behavior. At the other extreme, a proneness to experience fear or sadness without effective control may lead to more extreme negative moods and a risk for anxiety disorder and social phobia.

We must keep these differences in mind when considering developmental milestones in social and emotional behavior (see Table 3.1). Individual differences in the emotional response to social pressures and stress have a basis in the circuitry underlying response to negative and positive feedback in the environment. These differences can lead to important differences in social skills development and successful

Table 3.1. Age and Puberty-Related Social and Emotional Changes During Adolescence

Emotional	In early adolescence, there are increases in the following factors. • emotional reactivity • mood fluctuations • stress sensitivity • sexual interests • reward sensitivity, novelty seeking, and exploratory behavior (exploring boundaries of self and others) • more subject to "hot" cognition, particularly under the influence of peer pressure During late adolescence, there is an increased capacity to self-regulate emotional states.
Social	During early adolescence, there are increases in the following factors. • sense of self characterized by identity with specific group values and norms • sensitivity to peer evaluation, social acceptance and rejection, with peer evaluation playing an important role in determining self-worth • identity formation and separation from adult caregivers, although guidance is still needed from adult caregivers and role models • increased time spent with peers and developing peer relations During late adolescence, • peer evaluations become less important as a more coherent sense of self develops • the individual feels more comfortable choosing peer relationships and membership in groups that share similar values to those personally held • there is an increased ability to take another's perspective and to understand another's viewpoint • there is an increase in emotional (versus evaluative) empathy, but empathy becomes more evaluative in later adolescence

Also see Developing Adolescents: A Reference for Professionals. *American Psychological Association (2002).*
Available online http://www.apa.org/pi/families/resources/develop.pdf.

social interactions. They can also lead to differences in risk and resilience for psychopathology. Individual differences can arise from various sources, some of which will be addressed in the last section on genetics, environment, and their interaction.

3.4.1 Stress Sensitivity

We know from our earlier discussion that the stress hormone cortisol and stress system (HPA) activity increase around the time of puberty. The HPA system is responsible for preparing the body's defense system to react in stressful (e.g., threatening) situations. Studies have used various measures designed to increase stress during task performance in 9- to 15-year-olds[121] and in groups of children 7–12 years and 13–17 years of age.[257] The findings show that elevations of cortisol in response to stress increased with age and with puberty. Measures of heart rate also indicate that regulation of arousal increases with age.[121] The normal ramping up of the stress system enables adolescents to more effectively adapt to increasing challenges and demands as they explore their expanding social world. Research also implicates the sensitivity to social and emotional stressors in the development of psychopathology.[245] During adolescence, such sensitivity can be exceedingly problematic, when tools to effectively regulate increased arousal (e.g., frontal regions) are not fully mature. For example, girls who have higher temperament ratings of anxiety show greater cortisol response to stressors.[121] Similarly, anxious children become more sensitive to anxiety-producing stimuli after puberty.[213] Naturally, problems associated with stress sensitivity would be compounded if high-risk individuals are also immersed in high-stress psychosocial environments.

In general, studies with adults have indicated that high levels of stress are associated with adverse effects on health and mental functioning, causing, for example, sleeplessness, concentration problems, irritability, anxiety, and fatigue.[146,175] Although these findings are correlational in humans (see Box 3.3), animal studies have determined that stress can cause these problems and that effects of stress may be more detrimental during the adolescent period.

BOX 3.3 How to Study Individual Differences in Temperament

Correlational approaches are typically used to examine individual differences to assess the relationships between two variables.

Although relations between two variables may be found, this provides no information with respect to *causality*. For example, if decreases in amygdala activity are related to reduced anxiety, several interpretations could follow:

1. lower anxiety could result in decreased amygdala activity
2. decreased amygdala activity could result in decreased anxiety or
3. a third variable, such as maturation of prefrontal regions, may underlie the decrease in both variables.

Animal studies (for example, see Box 3.4) have indicated two main findings with respect to environmental stress during the adolescent period:[177,178]

- When adolescent animals are exposed to environmental stress, the reaction of the stress system lasts longer than in adult animals.
- A history of stress during early adolescence adversely affects the later development of cognitive and emotional systems (effects on learning and memory and increased anxiety-like behavior).

Recent human research examining chronically stressed adults has provided some insight into the mechanisms for stress-related difficulties in memory and attention.[57,146] Findings from this study suggest that environmental stress may alter the functional connections between the amygdala and prefrontal regions resulting in diminished ability to regulate emotions. Further research in this area is needed and will help us to understand the mechanisms underlying risk and resilience to psychopathology.

BOX 3.4 Social Stress in Adolescence Leads to Memory Impairments and Brain Alterations in Adulthood: An Animal Study

In this study, adolescent rats experienced 1 hour of isolation per day coupled with a daily change in cage mate. These rats showed a memory impairment compared with a control group only when they reached adulthood, long after the social stress period was over. Furthermore, this impairment and the adolescent stress experience were associated with chemical and neuronal growth changes in the hippocampus, the brain region associated with the particular memory challenge used. Thus, in contrast to research with adult animals, there appears to be an increased vulnerability to stressors specifically in adolescence, which affects ongoing brain development and results in reduced memory function in adulthood (see Ref. 178).

3.4.2 Implications

Although we are well aware of the adverse effects of environmental stress, it is important to keep in mind that adolescence may be a time of increased vulnerability to these effects. When we consider that there is a substantial increase in the incidence of depression, social anxiety, eating disorders, substance abuse and dependence, and schizophrenia during adolescence,[153] we should make every effort to minimize psychosocial stress over this period. We should also provide instruction to children on how to effectively cope with stress. Stress-reduction techniques have been shown not only to ameliorate the adverse effects of stress on health and cognitive functions, but they have also been associated with changes in brain activation patterns (see Box 3.5). Such techniques may help to reduce risk for mental disorders.

Research involving typically and atypically developing children and adolescents suggests that stress reduction techniques produce numerous positive changes, including reductions in emotional reactivity and anxiety and improvements in attention, executive function, and social skills.[36] Given the apparent efficacy of these techniques in altering brain structure and function in adults, it should be all the more effective when introduced, while the brain is still maturing and is open to healthy changes in its trajectory.

BOX 3.5 Stress Reduction Techniques

There are many stress reduction programs available (various meditation techniques, relaxation training methods, and self-hypnosis practices), which all share the same basic underlying philosophy: Reducing stress improves mental well-being and bodily immune function. The clinical application of these methods has been mostly, but not entirely, part of the so-called alternative medicine movement and part of nonwestern cultures for centuries if not millennia. However, medical documentation of the effectiveness of these techniques has occurred relatively recently. With new imaging technologies, neurobiological changes associated with such techniques have also been documented. Because controlled studies on the topic have occurred only recently, we must take all conclusions as needing further research for verification. However, the results to date appear to form a fairly reasonable and consistent story.

Mindfulness Training, or Mindfulness-Based Stress Reduction training, has been of particular interest to current medical and neuroscience researchers. The early clinical work from the 1980s and 1990s indicated that stress reduction was useful in treating disorders of affect, anxiety, and attention.[220] Furthermore, in a 4-month follow-up after an 8-week program of mindfulness meditation with healthy participants, there were significant changes (compared with the control group) in brain activation patterns that are normally related to positive affect and, as well, increases in antibody levels when challenged with a flu vaccine.[73] Similar results from a study in China reported greater improvement in mood, a decrease in cortisol (a stress hormone), and an increase in immunoreactivity.[261] Other clinical work with various meditation techniques has also found reduced relapses of depression in patients, reductions in blood pressure, and reductions in alcohol and substance abuse in prisoners.[55]

There have been a number of follow-up studies showing alterations in brain electrical activity (in the EEG) and increases in brain activation of the prefrontal cortex and the anterior cingulate (using fMRI).[55] A recent study with patients with social anxiety disorder indicated improvement in anxiety and self-esteem and reductions in amygdala activity and increases in regions associated with attention control.[117] Amygdala effects have been reported repeatedly in terms of both activity levels[133] and even in terms of gray matter density after only an 8-week intervention.[137] In another study by the same group, an 8-week program with healthy and meditation-naïve participants showed increased gray matter in brain regions involved in learning and memory, emotional regulation, and perspective taking.[138]

CHAPTER 4

How Genes and Environment Work Together to Influence Brain Growth and Behavior

As we have seen in previous chapters, the traditional view that the human brain reaches a near-mature state fairly early in childhood was incorrect. The major insight of the last decade is that there are sizable changes in structure and major changes in the balance of functioning as late as adolescence and early adulthood. The fact that we now have technologies to measure such changes relatively conveniently has allowed us to map their progression onto individual differences in personality and cognitive capacity, and to differences related to gender, hormones, and age. Given the knowledge we now have of structural changes during adolescence in gray matter, white matter, and in the functioning of some of the neurotransmitter systems, we will now examine what factors influence the trajectories of brain growth. We have already discussed some types of experiences that influence the outcome, but we can address this at a more mechanistic level by asking, "What actually guides the growth?" The basic answer in terms of mechanism is simple: genes. Brain growth and function are physically guided inevitably by genes, because genes contain the core information for the production of the proteins needed for the building blocks of brain tissue, hormones, and neurotransmitters. Therefore, when we ask why some brains grow differently and function differently from other brains, it would make sense to look for gene differences across people that produce these differing trajectories.

4.1 GENETIC EFFECTS ON BRAIN GROWTH

Genotype differences are characterized by variations in the structure of specific genes which are called *gene polymorphisms*. These multiple versions for each gene are called *alleles* (see Box 4.1 for definitions of terms). These polymorphisms result in brains that differ from each other in functional or structural details, and we call the brain outcomes *endophenotypes*. Research involving gene polymorphisms requires molecular analysis of the DNA of the research participants. Another method of relating genes to brain growth involves a measure called *heritability* that is derived from studies of family members, often of identical versus fraternal twins. One such study reported that the volume of white matter was more similar in identical twins than fraternal twins; that is, a significant amount of white matter growth is related to some aspect of the genotype.[53] Furthermore, those with more white matter (especially in the parietal region) also had a higher IQ score. The role of genes in this pattern was strengthened by finding that this relation between white matter and IQ was to a large extent accounted for by specific genes associated with the growth of white matter. In other words, the correlation between white matter growth and IQ was at least partly due to the genes involved in white matter growth.

When considering genetic effects on brain growth, it is important to note that the influences exerted by genes change across development and thus may differ depending on the developmental time point that is assessed. For example, heritability for language, tool use, and executive function is greater in adolescents than in children.[160] The influence of genes on brain development and function is not fixed! As we will see, changes in genetic influences over development are sometimes affected by environmental factors, so it becomes difficult to see genetic effects on the brain as completely separate from environmental effects (see Box 4.2).

BOX 4.1 Some Genetics Terms

Genotype: a specific complement of genes
Polymorphism: variation in a gene
Allele: a specific gene variant
Endophenotype: the resulting brain structure associated with a specific genotype
Heritability: the extent that trait variation across people is related to their genotype variation

BOX 4.2 Examples of Some Gene Effects on Brain Growth/Function

Gene	Effects	Reference
Androgen receptor gene	Gray matter density	202
MAO-A	Amygdala responsiveness Limbic volume Orbitofrontal cortex size Anterior cingulate function Aggressive behavior	182
COMT	Frontal cortex executive functions	274

Genotype variations also affect the dopamine and serotonin systems that play central roles in psychological traits and behaviors associated with mental health.[273,275] We know that these neurotransmitter systems have developmental trajectories themselves, and their influence on mental health and psychological traits changes as the person matures. Thus, it is not surprising that the genetic influence on psychological traits changes with age when the genetic effect occurs via these changing neurotransmitter systems. For example, as described earlier, there is a surge in growth of dopamine receptors during middle adolescence with the level reducing to adult levels in young adulthood. It turns out that the dopamine levels that are optimal for behavioral performance and control follow a "Goldilocks" pattern—not too low and not too high. This is the traditional inverted-U distribution. This has led researchers to compare the polymorphisms for a particular dopamine-related gene (called COMT) to see which is the best allele combination; that is, which one is associated with the top of the performance curve (see Figure 4.1). The genotype version associated with the best performance on some tasks in adults has the Met allele on both chromosomes, compared to people with the Val/Val variants. The Met/Val combination performs somewhere in between. One group of researchers reasoned that if the dopamine levels were increased too much, the Met/Met variant might become disadvantageous, as indicated in the left side of the figure.[274] Since we know that dopamine activation rises during adolescence, the combination that is at the optimal point in the curve should be different in adolescence, and indeed it is. Although adolescents with the Val/Met combination perform better on both tasks, the best adult performers are those with the Met/Met version (see Figure 4.2). Thus, particular gene combinations that give someone a performance advantage at one age

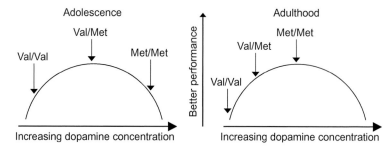

Fig. 4.1. *Theoretical illustration of how the inverted-U curve gives an advantage to the dopamine gene combinations (Val vs Met) when participants are tested on tasks related to prefrontal cortex functioning. In adulthood, reduced levels of dopamine cause all gene types to move to the left on the X-axis, changing the relative advantage of the various genotypes.* (*Source*: See Ref. 274.)

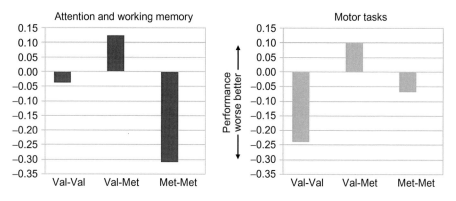

Fig. 4.2. *Neuropsychological performance pattern of dopamine gene combinations (Val vs Met) in adolescence (9–17 years). The Val-Met combination outperforms the other variants on both cognitive and motor tasks during this age period.* (*Source*: Data from Ref. 274.) (*See Plate 14*).

may disadvantage them at another, and therefore it is hard to conclude that one normal gene combination is "better" than another with respect to all contexts at all ages.

4.1.1 Experience Also Alters the Trajectory

There are now good demonstrations that experience can alter the gray and white matter organization in the cortex. This can happen simply through increased physical exercise that activates specific brain modules for movement such as the findings mentioned earlier: short-term practice at juggling alters gray matter mass;[81,82] extensive piano practice alters white matter;[21] the size of gray matter mass associated with finger control in violinists is a function of how long they have been playing and is specific to the left hand, which experiences the movement.[87] Sometimes the effects of experience are more subtle. For example, not only does socioeconomic status (SES) affect neurological and neuropsychological outcomes,[124,125,215] but also often alters the way genes affect brain outcomes (see Box 4.3). For example, the high level of heritability for white matter discussed earlier is for higher SES groups and drops in low SES groups.[54] Similarly, heritability for IQ is near zero when calculated from groups living in poverty but is very high for those in the upper middle classes.[269] Presumably this is because environmental influences on brain development increase when the person is in an at-risk context, but even when everything is going well (see Section 4.2), there is a ceiling to the positive effects of experience.

BOX 4.3 Some Interactions Between Socioeconomic Status (SES) or IQ and Genes in Brain Outcome

Effects of environmental adversity are conditional on an individual's genotype[179]

White matter (WM) volume is more heritable in higher SES[54]
80% of WM variation attributable to genes in above average IQ
40% of WM variation attributable to genes in below average IQ

SES alters the correlation between brain-derived neurotrophic factor (BDNF)-related genes and attention deficit hyperactivity disorder (ADHD) symptoms.[158] BDNF is brain-derived neurotrophic factor, a protein that is essential for certain neurotransmitters.
SES relates to a serotonin challenge more for some alleles of serotonin transporter[174]
Heritability of IQ near zero in poverty, and very high in higher SES[269]

Experience comes in many forms, and one can debate about whether what we call experience must come only through psychological channels of cognitive and interpersonal interactions. In the context of this discussion, where we are contrasting genetic sources of influence with environmental influences, we also need to consider the role of nongenetic biological factors that arise through specific environments. It comes as no surprise that these can alter the trajectory of brain growth, and hence of behavioral tendencies in adolescence. How they do so is a more complex story, as discussed in the next section in the case of nicotine.

4.1.1.1 Nicotine, an Example of a Brain-Trajectory Altering Drug
Drugs of addiction influence the adolescent brain differently from that of younger children or adults, and nicotine is a much-studied drug that illustrates the issues very well. High doses of nicotine are aversive to adults but not to adolescents, and adolescents are more sensitive to

the rewarding properties of nicotine. (See the paper by Dwyer and colleagues for a succinct review of animal and clinical literature.[84]) Thus, we know there are immediate effects on adolescent brains that put this age group at special risk, but what about long-term effects of early exposure on adolescent brain development?

We have known for a long time that smoking during pregnancy presents a health risk for the offspring, most reliably in terms of lower birth weight. However, we also know that there are more specific effects. Animal research has shown that, during the equivalent of the first and second trimesters of human prenatal growth, nicotine alters the growth of neurotransmitter systems with effects lasting through to adulthood. For example, early nicotine exposure can increase susceptibility to cocaine and other drugs of addiction, to ADHD, to conduct disorder and cognitive deficits (see Box 4.4).[84]

BOX 4.4 Prenatal Nicotine Alters Brain Development

Nicotine alters development of dopamine and norepinephrine pathways and brainstem nuclei associated with the autonomic nervous system (necessary for regulating heart and breathing functions, among others).

In the equivalent of the third trimester period, it alters development of the neocortex, hippocampus, and cerebellum.

Prenatal nicotine is associated with alterations in adolescent limbic system, dopamine and norepinephrine pathways.

Prenatal nicotine exposure can increase susceptibility to cocaine and other drugs of addiction, ADHD, conduct disorder, and cognitive deficits,[84] possibly due to a reduction in the volume and efficacy of the orbitofrontal cortex, raising the risk for drug experimentation in adolescence.

Some of these effects may be subject to interactions between specific genes and other environmental conditions.[149,163,191]

In a large-scale study of brain development, adolescents who were exposed to nicotine prenatally when compared with nonexposed control peers did not differ on a large battery of cognitive tests. However, they nevertheless did have reduced white matter joining the two hemispheres (in the corpus callosum) and had thinner gray matter in three regions, two of which are central to self-regulation, including the orbitofrontal cortex.[148,203,267] The thickness of the orbitofrontal cortex was also related to the adolescent participants' self-ratings on caring attitudes, a key component to positive mental health.

Of course, other drugs can affect brain growth, sometimes for the better. For example, in an animal study, researchers reversed stress-induced losses of synapses in the region critical for control over behavior with methylphenidate (Ritalin).[281] Such reversal strategies are of course tricky, and not often implemented in humans as a treatment. A much better strategy is to avoid the damaging trajectories in the first place.

4.1.2 Gene × Experience Interactions

It is clear from the example of early nicotine exposure that such a biological factor can have long-term consequences for adolescent mental health, and that the relations involved can become quite complex. Such a gene-by-environment interaction is illustrated in other developmental stressors as well, such as the experience of harsh, abusive, or neglectful upbringing that has now been shown to have biological effects just as explicitly ingested drugs. The effect of these stressors alters the hypothalamic pituitary adrenal (HPA) axis and the chemical balance in a way that affects major neurotransmitters. This has been documented in a well-publicized study of a dopamine-related gene that examined its interaction with experience. With normal nonabusive childhood experiences, the particular genotype is only mildly associated with violent behavior in adulthood. Without the particular gene polymorphism, experiencing an abusive childhood is similarly weakly associated with a violent temperament as an adult. However, when the particular polymorphism is paired with a highly stressed childhood, the probability of a violent or criminal outcome rises dramatically.[46]

Another example is how a particular serotonin gene variant puts the individual at risk for depression, but not when the environment is particularly supportive.[263] This kind of interaction of certain genotypes being at more risk in stressful environments is found repeatedly, emphasizing how the variation in genotypes across people increases the need to understand the interactions with the environment that they need for good mental health. Nevertheless, the same genotype is not a risk factor in healthy environments and it may even be advantageous. Thus the gene is not the risk factor per se, but rather its combination with specific environments puts the person at risk.

4.1.3 What is the Mechanism for the "Trainable" Brain?

The recent popularity of books and articles on how the brain is "trainable" further pushes the search for mechanisms of this flexibility in brain growth.[79] To understand the mechanism, we turn again to genes. When genes are activated (i.e., are turned on), they produce proteins that are used in building the body and in its functions. They are not continually active, but rather produce the proteins needed when they are called upon. The activation of genes is controlled by a complex chemical sequence involving hormones, whose production and dispersal into the blood stream is highly influenced by experience, both psychological and physical. This process by which genes are turned on and off is called *epigenetics*, and it forms the basis for our real understanding of how nature and nurture intertwine in development (see Box 4.5). Thus, genes map onto the processes that influence brain function, but the brain's experience also influences the genetic activation. This interplay between genetics and environment is currently the most challenging area for developmental neuroscience (see Figure 4.3). Although we cannot go into detail here, we can see that this is the mechanism for gene-by-environment interactions and for understanding how environment influences brain growth (especially with respect to stressful environments). There are far too many factors for there to be a simple effect of either genes or environment to account for all the variation in outcomes. Having a specific gene provides only probabilities concerning outcomes, just as having a specific experience only increases the likelihood of success or failure at a task.

BOX 4.5 Epigenetics

"… behavioral development is thought to result from the interplay among genetic inheritance, congenital characteristics, cultural contexts, and parental practices as they directly impact the individual… [A]nother contributor, *epigenetic inheritance*, [is] the transmission to offspring of parental phenotypic responses to environmental challenges—even when the young do not experience the challenges themselves. Genetic inheritance is not altered, gene expression is… Maternal stress during the latter half of a daughter's gestation may affect not only the daughter's but also grand-offspring's physical growth… temperamental variation may be influenced in the same way."[128, p 340]

One of the recent findings in epigenetics is that patterns of gene regulation can be passed down across generations, adding a further

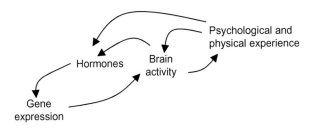

Fig. 4.3. *Epigenetics captures the interplay between genes and experience. Genetic expression is necessary for brain activity, but that expression is regulated partly by what the brain experiences.*

complication to the story. It turns out the influence of inheritance from the mother and father is not simply the gene types received, but also their influence on gene expression (this is called *imprinting*).

4.1.4 Adolescence-Specific Epigenetic Effects

One of the interesting logical conclusions we can draw from the picture so far is that because there are biological changes such as puberty starting during adolescence, then there must be a different pattern of genes active during adolescence. Indeed, an examination of almost 10,000 genes in the rat brain shows dramatic differences in the timing of their activity in 97% of them.[247] An obvious example of this in adolescence is a behavior change associated with puberty, that of eating, where the degree to which individuals increase their intake varies considerably: Genetic variation accounts for far more variation in eating behavior during puberty (54%) than prepubertally (about 0%), whereas heritability in pubertal 11-year-olds was about the same as that in 17-year-olds.[154] So some genes must be accounting for eating behavior because of the high heritability, but their influence interacts with the age at which they are being examined. Similarly, a meta-analysis showed that, between ages 13 and 35, heritability increased for mental health concerns of anxiety symptoms, depression symptoms, alcohol consumption, externalizing behavior, social attitudes, and nicotine initiation, but there was no increase for ADHD.[22] In other words, the size of heritability depends on the age group examined for some traits more than others.

This has implications for understanding the sources of adolescent behavior. We know that some risk behaviors and mental health concerns increase during the adolescent period, but that gene-related influence also increases during this period for some mental health concerns and not others. Therefore, the increase in risk behavior and mental health concerns during adolescence are not simply due to increased peer influences, unless susceptibility to that influence is also heritable. This is one of the ways in which addressing behavior change may be more complicated during this period than before or afterwards.

4.2 A BROAD RANGE OF EXPERIENTIAL FACTORS INFLUENCE BRAIN DEVELOPMENT

There is a wide range of factors associated with variable brain development. These can be divided broadly into positive and negative effects. The evidence for the negative effects is much stronger for two reasons: (1) Threats to healthy growth are more likely to be the target of research funding, with more agencies and researchers devoted to removing developmental dangers and obstacles. (2) Given our relatively affluent and open society, children are stimulated well enough in the average environment that it may be difficult to find ways to visibly improve brain development, even when behavioral improvements of an educational or social nature are evident. In addition, researchers are not always able to articulate whether a minor alteration in the trajectory is in fact beneficial or not, or is simply a change that adds to individuality in our society. However, some negative aspects of experience are obviously worrisome, and we will discuss these first.

4.2.1 Stress

The most studied effect of experience on brain growth is that of stressors (see Chapter 3). Early animal work demonstrated that mild stress experiences are beneficial for normal brain development, in that these mimic the normal wild environment in which they develop. This includes being exposed to visual, tactile and other sensory novel objects, and to having to deal socially with others. Deprivation of these experiences hinders normal brain development in a variety of ways.[222] The important question concerns major stressors, equivalent to physical or psychological abuse or neglect. As we discussed earlier, there is now plenty of evidence from animal studies that early major stressors alter the developmental trajectory of the brain. Whether isolated major stress experience during late childhood and adolescence in humans can alter the trajectory from its normal pathway is harder to document. However, experiences inducing post-traumatic stress disorder (PTSD) in childhood or adulthood can alter physiological responses,[32,270] and animal work has shown clear changes in the fear circuitry of the brain as a result of stress experiences even in adult rats.[183,272]

4.2.2 Video Games and Digital Media

Other recreational activities have been explored in terms of effects on brain function, with much publicity, for example, on effects of intensive video game playing. Some positive cognitive and perceptual effects have been shown in the laboratory to be attributable to game playing.[15,151] Some negative effects on attention skills as a function of those who play more versus less in their normal lives have also been documented.[24,105] In addition, greater psychological distress in 10- and 11-year-olds has been documented for those who have more television or computer time irrespective of physical activity.[196] There are also some laboratory results showing reduced cortical connectivity after playing violent video games.[278] There are also potential negative aspects of heavy internet use.[41,194] Thus, evaluating the effects of being connected to the digital world, as many young people are, is complex and involves many potential factors, above and beyond intensive playing of video games.[14]

4.2.3 Physical Health Threats

We discussed earlier the research on prenatal nicotine affecting later development, including effects showing up in adolescence. There are other major factors that have been documented, some better than others.

4.2.3.1 Air Pollution

The issue of particulate matter in the air is fast becoming a major concern in the medical community. It is estimated to be already responsible for thousands of deaths a year in a jurisdiction with a population of only 11 million,[40] mainly of older adults, due to its effects on heart function and respiration illnesses. However, there are also effects on the brain because the fine particles can invade brain tissue and initiate an inflammatory response. Thus, there is the possibility of major effects on children's brains as well. Although this work needs to be replicated, one research team has reported that the major air pollution in Mexico City is responsible for white matter lesions in the frontal lobe regions

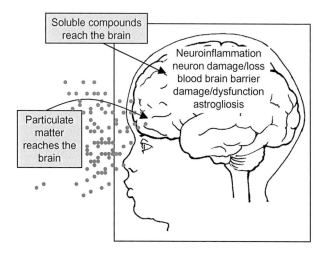

Fig. 4.4. Air pollution containing fine particulate matter with particles smaller than 2.5 μm (PM2.5) can penetrate into the exchange of gas in the lungs. Some research suggests that these small particles are capable of crossing the blood-brain barrier, leading to inflammation and damage in the brain (Source: See Ref. 31.) (See Plate 15).

of children, possibly accounting for the poorer intellectual performance they found in the sample[31] (see Figure 4.4). Although it is acknowledged that Mexico City has one of the worst air pollution records, the effect should be simply cumulative, with any serious pollution being a concern for the health of developing brains.

4.2.3.2 Toxins and Drug Exposure

Substance abuse during adolescence is well documented, and is discussed earlier in this chapter. Given the clear evidence of continuing brain development until early adulthood, we should expect that substance abuse would affect brain growth. Documenting this in humans is of course difficult because substance abuse correlates with other lifestyle factors that could also be detrimental to brain growth. However, the evidence is fairly convincing. For example, binge drinking in adolescence is associated with reduced white matter in 18 brain regions and not with increases in any region. The white matter volumes were linearly related to blood alcohol concentrations during the previous 3 months and to the intensity of the drinking.[181] More serious toxins and substance abuse have more severe neurological effects.[167] This is suggestive of a causal relation. However, there are sometimes age-specific effects that need to be further researched. For example, a study recently found that adolescent rats were relatively unaffected by binge toluene inhalation, whereas rats in the young adult stage were seriously affected.[192] Thus, there may be age-specific effects as well as general effects, and sorting out the age-specific effects may streamline intervention strategies.

4.2.3.3 Concussion

Concussion is often thought of as a very mild brain insult, so mild in fact that usually there are no long-term implications. This is often (although not always) the case for a first concussion. However, the effects of concussion are cumulative and can be very severe. The issue has been in the public view lately because of a growing awareness of the number of concussions occurring in professional sports, sometimes completely altering the career path of promising young athletes. More recently, there has been public discussion about the incidence of concussions among children and adolescents in organized sports. We should first point out that one of the best predictors of someone incurring a head injury is a history of having already received one. This could be for several reasons. In general, those with a risky style of playing sports or recreational activities may be at higher risk. However, concussion and mild traumatic brain injury (TBI) compromise those regions of the brain highly involved in quick judgment and coordination, namely the frontal lobe. The frontal lobe is at risk during head injury because of the structure of the skull and the structure of brain injury due to movement of the brain within the skull. Given these risk factors, especially in the context of a growing brain, we should be highly concerned about a high incidence of concussion in children and adolescents. Furthermore, some of this is under our control. A large Canadian study documented the incidence of injuries in general and concussions in particular among 11- and 12-year-old children in organized hockey in Alberta and Quebec. There were more than 2.5 times as many injuries in general and 3.3 times as many concussions in the Alberta players.[88] In Quebec, there is no body checking allowed in this age group, whereas there is body checking in Alberta (see Figure 4.5). Although hockey enthusiasts insist that body checking must be allowed at some stage of play, we can question whether this has to be during a period of important brain development.

This issue is especially apparent in a recent study concerning the effects of concussion among early (9–12-year-old) and mid (13–16-year-old) adolescent and adult athletes, all compared to control groups matched for age and sex.[11] The researchers examined cognitive functions and cortical brain wave responses (using *event-related potentials*) an average of 6 months after injury. The startling finding was that despite a lack of cognitive

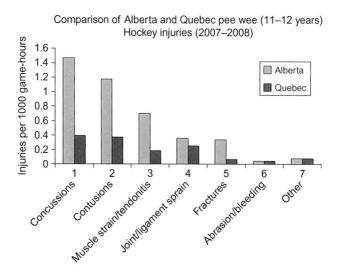

Fig. 4.5. A comparison of injuries incurred during pee-wee hockey games when cross-checking is allowed (Alberta) versus not allowed (Quebec). (Source: Data from Ref. 88.) (See Plate 16).

symptoms in general, the 13–16-year-olds were the only ones to show a deficit on any of the seven assessment measures, namely one specifically related to working memory. Furthermore, these adolescents showed a 24% reduction in the P300 component of the event-related potential, a standard electrical brain response component that is associated with attention control. There was a much smaller reduction in the children, and no significant difference in the adults. Thus, behavioral testing did not pick up the serious reduction in brain electrical response associated with attention that remained 6 months after the concussion, putting the athlete at continued risk if he/she returned to play. Although we do not yet know the long-term implications for brain health, these results highlight how behavioral testing alone does not reflect the full implications of concussion for children and especially for adolescents.

4.2.4 Giving Brain Development an Advantage
4.2.4.1 Exercise
There is much research with older adults on the benefits of exercise for cognition and the brain, and considerable animal research showing benefits in brain function from exercise.[284] It has even been demonstrated in older adults that random assignment to an exercise regime increases brain activity and volume in frontal and temporal lobes.[156] However,

the research literature concerning children and adolescents on the effects of exercise on brain growth is still relatively sparse. What we do know is that there is much evidence that increased physical exercise in childhood and adolescence is associated in general with increased academic performance and cognitive skills despite the reduced classroom time because of the time taken for the exercise activities.[235,268] The few brain studies that have been done with children are supportive of a positive effect. High-fit 9-year-olds were found to produce larger electrocortical brain responses in an attention task than low-fit children of the same age[135] and to perform better on memory and executive control tasks.[51] Similarly in 9–10-year-olds, aerobic fitness is correlated with a specific type of memory (called relational memory) and with greater volume of gray matter in the brain region (the hippocampus) most related to this form of memory.[49] Aerobic fitness is also correlated with attention skills and their associated brain regions.[50]

There are starting to be true experimental research designs with children involving randomized assignment to exercise conditions. These controlled studies are needed in order to conclude that it is the exercise that is producing the results. The studies have shown that children in general benefit from an exercise program. For example, a 6-month after-school 2-hour program for 7–9-year-olds resulted in an increase in cardiovascular fitness. It also improved memory performance and led to a more mature electrical brain response in the frontal lobe.[150] This was also true for young adolescents (7–11 years) who are inactive and overweight but otherwise healthy.[74,75] Not only was this short-term intervention (such as 20 or 40 minutes per day for 13 weeks) effective at raising executive function and cognitive performance, but also it shifted the balance of brain activation to the prefrontal cortex from parietal cortex during a task requiring good control (see Figure 4.6).

There is some controversy still as to whether simple exercise alone is enough to boost executive functions or whether complex tasks involving exercise, such as those involving others as in team sports or choreographed dancing, are needed.[23]

4.2.4.2 Educational Experiences
There are many social and educational experiences that are seen as beneficial for child development. There is also some discussion nowadays as to whether the social and educational experiences have similar beneficial

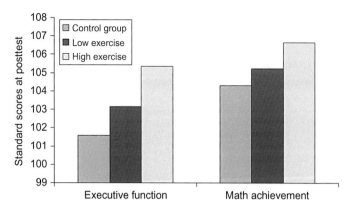

Fig. 4.6. The effects on executive function and math achievement of a 13-week after-school low (20 min per day) and high (40 min per day) aerobic exercise program for 7–11-year-olds. (Source: Data from Ref. 74.) (See Plate 17).

effects in brain growth and function, beyond those associated with physical exercise as described earlier. Favorite topics include music lessons, second language acquisition, and executive function training. There are many studies comparing musicians and nonmusicians on brain structures and cognitive skills, and no doubt the intense experience that professionals undergo will have some effects on brain growth (beyond the movement-related gray matter changes mentioned earlier). However, it is very difficult to separate out confounding factors in such studies in order to isolate what it is about being a musician that leads to such effects. Nevertheless, some studies have examined short-term effects of music lessons on children's brains, demonstrating that there are effects that can be measured even in these limited circumstances.[100,141] Similarly, in a behavioral study, having music lessons has been reported to increase the IQ slightly (with drama lessons increasing social skills).[223] Unfortunately, the long-term effects of these changes on brain development are not yet known.

Similarly, there is excitement in the field concerning potential benefits of bilingualism on developing executive functions.[25–27,29] However, as with sampling already accomplished musicians, there may be other factors associated with having a second language that affect executive functions in children,[186] although researchers do try to control for the other factors. The similarity in benefits of musical training and second language acquisition has also been explored in terms of cognitive skills.[28] Thus, it is certainly possible that the focused attention and disciplined thinking that is required for musical training or learning a second language may have measurable effects on brain development, but more research is needed to document exactly how such effects might work.

Throughout this book, we have emphasized the critical role of stress, being a positive factor if a short-term challenge, and being a negative factor if prolonged or chronic. The earlier discussion of meditation as a stress reduction technique points to a specific strategy that is available for healthier brain growth.

4.3 IMPLICATIONS: THE BOTTOM LINE

The overall message we can take from the current research on adolescent brain development should not excessively surprise anyone who has worked with children and youth, or indeed raised them in a family context. We have always known that growing up to adult maturity is a long process. However, we can now document that this is not just a function of the time needed to have experiences and learn about how the world works and how other people behave. It is also that experiences during growth affect the healthy unfolding of brain structures. Of course, it is those brain structures that are central to how the child or adolescent interprets the experiences, resulting in a feedback loop that is essential to our understanding of mental health. We have presented evidence of many threats to healthy brain growth, but have also discussed some ways to accentuate positive factors. One such factor that has not yet been related to specifics of brain structure and function, but clearly must be related in some way, is captured by the notion of "engagement." There is a resurgence in this concept in the research literature on adolescence, and it can be summarized by thinking about the benefits of being passionately absorbed in constructive activities. Adolescents who are positively engaged demonstrate higher academic performance, happiness, and general psychological well-being.[98] Such engaged living is associated with fewer psychological maladies, such as depression, anxiety, substance abuse and violent behaviors.[68,176] As adults, our responsibility for healthy brain growth among our youth is to foster contexts in which such positive processes are enabled and threats are minimized.

SUMMARY

The brain continues to organize, adapt, and change well beyond the early years, and, in some respects, over the full lifespan. The changes that occur over late childhood, adolescence, and into young adulthood are particularly dramatic and occur at all levels: molecular, cellular, anatomical, and functional. During this important stage of brain development, the processes involved in the remodeling and shaping of brain structure and neural circuitry are thought to contribute to the behavioral changes that are often noted across cultures during the adolescent period (e.g., increased risk-taking behavior, novelty seeking, and increased affiliation with peers).

The substantial changes occurring in the brain over this period are discussed below.

Cortical Changes
- Overall, gray matter (neuronal cell bodies, dendrites, and glial cells) development follows an inverted-U pattern of growth, first thickening in volume, peaking, and then thinning.
- Gray matter increases or "thickens" until around the onset of puberty (11 years for girls, 12 years for boys) and then begins to decrease or "thin" as excess synapses are pruned or eliminated.
- The pruning of excess synapses is thought to follow a "use it or lose it" policy. The synapses that are used are strengthened and maintained and those that are not used as frequently are lost.
- Gray matter maturation follows a nonlinear pattern and proceeds in a back-to-front manner—first in brain regions underlying sensory systems and movement and lastly in regions that integrate this information, including the frontal regions involved in planning, strategizing, and goal setting.
- The process of synaptic pruning is thought to enhance the efficiency of neuronal processing. This leads to a brain that is more economical because less energy is required to maintain synapses that are not used frequently.

• This pruning process is dramatic over the adolescent period, and research strongly implicates the role of experience in this process.

White Matter Changes

• White matter increases in a roughly linear pattern throughout childhood, adolescence, and into young adulthood. Development proceeds first from regions of the brain responsible for sensation and movement, then in areas related to memory, spatial orientation and the comprehension of language, and lastly in the frontal regions involved in impulse control, goal setting, and other executive functions.
• The process of myelination, which speeds up the communication between nerve cells in the brain, shows dramatic changes during this period. One important aspect of myelination is that as its completion takes place in particular brain regions, it actually limits the brain's ability to adapt to environmental influences. During adolescence, in certain brain regions, the amount of myelin doubles. Thus, this is an extremely important time for experience-induced changes on brain development, especially in pathways that are responsible for the voluntary control of behavior.
• Over childhood, adolescence, and young adulthood, white matter connections between brain regions are reorganizing and strengthening. The maturation of white matter over this period allows for more efficient transfer of information and the refinement of higher order cognitive processes, such as attention, working memory, and self-regulation.
• Research strongly implicates the role of experience in white matter development.

Changes in Connections Between Brain Regions

• There is now a general consensus that the brain doesn't mature in stages that depend on the development of specific regions, but rather that maturation reflects the emergence and refinement of networks.
• Many changes occur in the connections between brain regions. Brain imaging studies have shown that in younger children, the brain processes information in a more locally distributed and less efficient manner. This type of processing is replaced with more focused and efficient processing as the brain develops. Brain regions and the pathways connecting them become more specialized.
• As long-range connections increase and specialized brain networks develop, the workload of cognitive processing becomes more widely

distributed and integrated with more distant brain regions. This leads to increased resources and more efficient processing.

Brain Changes Involved in Social and Emotional Behavior

- Subcortical regions involved in the processing of emotion mature earlier than prefrontal regions that regulate decision making, planning, and impulse control.
- This mismatch of maturation rates for regions involved in behavioral control and those involved in emotional reactivity is thought to contribute to the noted behavioral changes that occur with the onset of puberty and during the transition into adolescence.
- Such changes include increases in thrill-seeking and risk-taking behavior, increased emotionality, and fluctuations in mood.
- Research has shown that risk-taking behavior is more strongly related to puberty than to age. On the other hand, voluntary control of behavior is more strongly related to age than to puberty. This leads to a very sensitive transition point. When puberty begins, the sensitivity to rewards is peaking, a time when cognitive control is relatively immature.
- Changes in behavior occurring over this period are paralleled by changes in brain responses. For example, there is increased activity in the brain regions involved in emotion during adolescence, especially in the regions responsible for the processing of pleasure and reward.
- During early adolescence, when emotional reactivity increases and control regions are still immature, some adolescents may find it more difficult to self-regulate and to put off immediate rewards in the service of long-term goals. There is also an increased response to stress during this time and risk for mental health issues.
- Dramatic alterations are also taking place within the brain's neurotransmitter systems. Such changes, which have been most widely studied in the dopamine system, have implications for the brain's response to rewarding stimuli in the environment, with further implications for novelty seeking and risk-taking behavior, including susceptibility to drug abuse.
- Research in other areas of social development have shown that the brain regions and circuitry involved in the perception of facial emotions, taking other people's perspective, and empathic responding are also not fully mature until adulthood.

Genetic and Environmental Influences

- The interplay of genetics and experience is complex: Genes are central to the building and functioning of the brain, but their regulation and expression is heavily influenced by experience.
- Genes that control certain aspects of brain development occur at different times across the development, with some becoming active earlier in childhood and others later, including during the adolescent period.
- Some gene combinations may be associated with better performance on some tasks at one age and poorer performance at another. It is not usually possible to consider a particular gene as being better than another (unless it is associated with a clear medical illness).
- We can best think of genes as providing a predisposition to respond to environmental influences, although also keeping in mind that the environment exerts important influences on which genes are expressed and how they are expressed.
- The regulation and expression of specific genes involved in brain development changes over time and the influence of experiences (whether enriching or adverse) also changes with age and with circumstances. There are individual differences in behavior that are traceable in a general fashion to gene patterns that affect important chemicals in the brain, such as dopamine or serotonin.

IMPLICATIONS FOR POLICYMAKERS

There are a number of key points for policymakers from this body of scientific evidence. These points (and the literature summary) were originally addressed to those asking for policy implications arising from the research field of adolescent brain development. Some of these points reinforce already existing policy that sometimes reflects longstanding approaches to youth services. Other points reflect what we feel are misconceptions in some jurisdictions as to the best way to deal with problems of youth care. Yet other points simply summarize the main conceptual issues that should be driving policy decisions.

1. Brain changes from late childhood into early adulthood are not hard-wired. There is considerable adaptability and plasticity in the brain's structure and function. The maturation process is influenced by genetics and multiple environmental factors and their interactions. There is accumulating evidence that individual differences in brain

development may be linked to experience. Whether the developing child/adolescent spends considerable time engaging in sports, video games, negotiating family stress, or taking illicit drugs matters and may have long-lasting effects on how the brain is wired. This time of brain plasticity suggests that not only is this a period of vulnerability to adverse environmental influences, but also it is a time of opportunity. Prevention and intervention can enhance positive brain growth and development.

2. During adolescence, frontal networks involved in "executive control" functions are not fully mature. When an adolescent is performing tasks and activities that involve executive functions, such as organizing, strategizing, planning, or regulating emotion, there is an increased chance that he or she will be operating at full capacity. Additional stressors in the environment, whether unexpected or ongoing, may lead to impaired behavior and choices. One such stressor is sleep deprivation. A sleep-deprived adolescent starts the day with a reduction in these executive capacities. Such negative effects may be increased due to the changes in sleep cycles that come normally with the onset of puberty. Teens need guidance and support from parents and community with respect to these limitations, especially in stress-related contexts.

3. The brain circuitry supporting self-regulation and the control of emotions is still forming over the adolescent period. There is speculation that experience with effective self-regulation will strengthen and improve the functioning of this brain circuitry. To maximize the likelihood of success, children should learn strategies for effective self-regulation early in development and these strategies should be continually reinforced, especially around the onset of puberty and during early adolescence.

4. Children and adolescents have not reached the adult levels of processing efficiency in the brain networks supporting social cognition despite apparent sophistication in some contexts. The circuitry supporting mature levels of perspective taking and empathic understanding have not fully matured. It is important that policies take into account the normal developmental timeline of these mental processes.

5. Adolescents make some decisions as well as adults do, and they appear highly competent in calm contexts. However, there is increasing evidence to show that this is not the case when adolescents are in emotional contexts, such as when they are excited and with peers.

Decision making can be quite impaired during such "hot" contexts, with adolescents showing a greater propensity for immediate reward and less consideration of long-term consequences. Considering that much adolescent misbehavior is done in a social context, this has implications for forensic issues related to young offenders. This is an issue of some discussion in the legal system in the USA concerning taking into account issues relating to diminished capacity for decision making during adolescence.[250,251]

6. Adolescents compared to adults are more sensitive to social evaluations and yet are less able to effectively regulate the emotions surrounding such evaluations because their frontal brain regions are not fully mature. Adolescence is also a time when sensitivity to peer evaluation increases and seems to be more influential in determining concepts of self-worth. These factors are especially important considering that adolescence is a time of increased risk-taking behavior and increased risk for the emergence of psychopathology.

7. Adolescence is a time of heightened propensity for reward-seeking and risk-taking behavior, characterized by an emphasis on short-term goals and discounting future implication. Given the vulnerability at this stage of development, we can be sure that outcomes will be heavily dependent on guidance from parents, adult role models and institutions. Reward-seeking behavior is a part of healthy social development. Thus, guidance should include providing ample opportunities for adolescents to engage in positive reward-seeking behaviors, so that they will have alternatives that help them avoid expressing these drives in negative contexts.

8. When puberty begins, the sensitivity to rewards is at its peak, a time when cognitive control is relatively immature. This imbalance may become even more of a societal focus if the age of puberty onset continues to recede, as it has for over a century. The timing of these changes may have implications for interventions designed to reduce adolescent risk-taking behavior.

9. Brain changes over this developmental period increase vulnerability to stress, putting some youth at increased risk for psychopathology. High levels of stress are also known to influence the trajectory of the brain growth in negative ways. It is important to make every effort to minimize psychosocial stress, providing community and family support when needed. This can be done by making instruction in relaxation and stress-reduction techniques readily available to developing youth so that they can exercise some control over their

stress levels. Stress-reduction techniques not only ameliorate the adverse effects of stress on health and cognitive functions, but they have also been associated with positive changes in brain activation and growth patterns. Given the apparent efficacy of these techniques in altering brain structure and function in adults, it should be all the more effective when introduced although the brain is still maturing and is open to healthy changes in trajectory.

10. With the onset of puberty, there is an increase of substance abuse during adolescence[200] but the long-term impact on the developing brain is still unclear. However, evidence suggests that adverse effects of drugs on brain structure and function may be different for adolescents compared to adults. Heavy drinking during adolescence may make the person particularly prone to adverse effects on brain structure and cognitive function.[120] Cannabis use in adolescence may contribute to, rather than cause, an increased risk of psychosis given that those at risk for psychosis may be self-medicating at a premorbid stage.[12,132] Considering what we know about brain plasticity during this time, prevention and intervention programs for drug abuse should be readily available to developing youth.

11. There is much evidence that physical exercise is associated in general with increased academic performance and cognitive skills. Aerobic fitness has been related to memory performance and also to greater volume of gray matter in the brain region most involved in memory (the hippocampus) and with attention skills and their associated brain regions. Exercise programs should be encouraged not only for their general health benefits, but also because they may influence positive brain growth.

12. There are many social and educational experiences that are seen as beneficial for child development, and there is some evidence that these have positive growth effects on the brain. Candidate activities include learning a second language and participating in organized music lessons.

13. The frontal lobe is at risk during head injury because of the internal structure of the skull and the structure of brain injury due to movement of the brain within the skull. Given these risk factors, especially in the context of a growing brain, we should be very concerned about a high incidence of preventable concussion in children and adolescents. Some of this is under our control in terms of encouraging or discouraging violent or aggressive behavior in contact sports.

14. Prenatal nicotine exposure can alter the trajectory of the growth of some neurotransmitter systems such that there is an increased susceptibility to cocaine and other drugs of addiction, to attention deficit hyperactivity disorder (ADHD), to conduct disorder and cognitive deficits later in development. Prenatal counseling of young mothers should emphasize the seriousness of the risk for these long-term mental health issues.

15. There is considerably more brain adaptability and vulnerability during younger years in comparison to adulthood. For this reason, rehabilitation programs for antisocial behavior are more appropriate than incarceration for two reasons. First, adolescents learn better when responding to rewards than by avoiding behaviors because of punishments; that is, the lessons are more likely to be well learned. This speaks as well to the problem of long-term incarceration leading to more ingrained antisocial behaviors. Second, stress is a major negative epigenetic influence on brain growth, and therefore sustained high stress levels are much more likely to worsen self-regulation and adaptability than to promote good behavior.

16. While there are hereditary effects influencing behavioral development, these effects can be greater or lesser during adolescence compared to childhood and adulthood. This means that what is seen as a biologically heritable pattern of behavior, for example related to temperament, at one age might nonetheless be strongly influenced by experience at another age. Thus, one should never assume that genetic predispositions are unchangeable. Conversely, we may find that some individuals who have been apparently blessed with a good behavioral repertoire, learned through a positive family and peer context, can nonetheless fall prey to genetically heritable influences during adolescence that did not seem to be operating earlier.

17. The evidence for increased brain responses during adolescence in emotional contexts is clear. However, this increase is also accompanied by a wider range of responses, indicating that only a portion of adolescents show responses dramatically different from those of younger children or adults. This has implications for any context that generalizes to all adolescents. The vulnerability of this period encourages caregivers to protect adolescents from potential dangers, but many individuals are able to handle stressors as well as adults, and just as healthily. Therefore, it is also important to use judgment to not overgeneralize.

18. A potential general threat to healthy brain development is air pollution. Government policies on pollution are often almost exclusively

driven by fiscal considerations. This leads to considerably higher particulate matter in the air than is healthy. Although this is especially important for the health of older adults, driving up medical costs in this cohort, it may also be affecting the healthy growth of our children's brains. The available evidence suggests that exactly those brain regions central to self-regulation are the ones most at risk from inflammation due to particulate matter invading the brain.

REFERENCES

1. Albert D, Steinberg L, Banich M (2009) Age differences in strategic planning as indexed by the Tower of London. *Child Dev* **80**, 28–44.
2. Albert D, Steinberg L (2011) Judgment and decision making in adolescence. *J Res Adolesc* **21**, 211–224.
3. Allen JS, Damasio H, Grabowski TJ *et al.* (2003) Sexual dimorphism and asymmetries in the gray-white composition of the human cerebrum. *Neuroimage* **18**, 880–894.
4. Andersen SL, Dumont NL, Teicher MH (1997) Developmental differences in dopamine synthesis inhibition by (±)-7-OH-DPAT. *N Schmied Arch Pharmacol* **356**, 173–181.
5. Arnett J (1992) Reckless behavior in adolescence: A developmental perspective. *Dev Rev* **12**, 339–373.
6. Arnett J (1994) Sensation seeking: A new conceptualization and a new scale. *Pers Indiv Differ* **16**, 289–296.
7. Asato MR, Terwilliger R, Woo J *et al.* (2010) White matter development in adolescence: A DTI study. *Cereb Cortex* **20**, 2122–2131.
8. Ashtari M, Cervellione KL, Hasan KM *et al.* (2007) White matter development during late adolescence in healthy males: a cross-sectional diffusion tensor imaging study. *Neuroimage* **35**(2), 501–510.
9. Baars BJ, Gage NM (2010) *Cognition, Brain, and Consciousness: An Introduction to Cognitive Neuroscience* (2nd ed.). San Diego: Academic Press.
10. Baddeley AD (1986) *Working Memory*. Oxford: Oxford University Press.
11. Baillargeon A, Lassonde M, Leclerc S *et al.* (2012) Neuropsychological and neurophysiological assessment of sport concussion in children, adolescents and adults. *Brain Inj* **26**, 211–220.
12. Barkus E, Murray RM (2010) Substance use in adolescence and psychosis: clarifying the relationship. *Annu Rev Clin Psychol* **6**, 365–389.
13. Barnea-Goraly N, Menon V, Eckert M *et al.* (2005) White matter development during childhood and adolescence: a cross-sectional diffusion tensor imaging study. *Cereb Cortex* **15**, 1848–1854.
14. Bavelier D, Green CS, Dye MW (2010) Children, wired: for better and for worse. *Neuron* **67**, 692–701.
15. Bavelier D, Levi DM, Li RW *et al.* (2010) Removing brakes on adult brain plasticity: from molecular to behavioral interventions. *J Neurosci* **30**, 14964–14971.
16. Beltran I, Chassin L, Hussong, A (2009) Adolescent substance use. In *Handbook of adolescent psychology*, 3rd ed. pp. 723–764 [ML Lerner, L Steinberg, editors]. New York: John Wiley.
17. Ben Bashat D, Ben Sira L, Graif M *et al.* (2005) Normal white matter development from infancy to adulthood: comparing diffusion tensor and high b value diffusion weighted MR images. *J Magn Reson Imaging* **21**, 503–511.
18. Benes FM (1989) Myelination of cortical-hippocampal relays during late adolescence. *Schizophr Bull* **15**, 585–593.
19. Benes FM (1998) Brain development, VII. Human brain growth spans decades. *Am J Psychiatry* **155**, 1489.
20. Benes FM, Turtle M, Khan Y *et al.* (1994) Myelination of a key relay zone in the hippocampal formation occurs in the human brain during childhood, adolescence, and adulthood. *Arch Gen Psychiatry* **51**, 477–484.
21. Bengtsson SL, Nagy Z, Skare S *et al.* (2005) Extensive piano practicing has regionally specific effects on white matter development. *Nat Neurosci* **8**, 1148–1150.
22. Bergen SE, Gardner CO, Kendler KS (2007) Age-related changes in heritability of behavioral phenotypes over adolescence and young adulthood: a meta-analysis. *Twin Res Hum Genet* **10**, 423–433.
23. Best JR (2010) Effects of physical activity on children's executive function: contributions of experimental research on aerobic exercise. *Dev Rev* **30**, 331–551.

24. Beullens K, Roe K, VandenBulck J (2011) Excellent gamer, excellent driver? The impact of adolescents' video game playing on driving behavior: a two-wave panel study. *Accid Anal Prev* **43**, 58–65.
25. Bialystok E (1999) Cognitive complexity and attentional control in the bilingual mind. *Child Dev* **70**, 636–644.
26. Bialystok E, Craik FI, Grady C *et al.* (2005) Effect of bilingualism on cognitive control in the Simon task: evidence from MEG. *Neuroimage* **24**, 40–49.
27. Bialystok E, Craik FI, Klein R *et al.* (2004) Bilingualism, aging, and cognitive control: evidence from the Simon task. *Psychol Aging* **19**, 290–303.
28. Bialystok E, Depape AM (2009) Musical expertise, bilingualism, and executive functioning. *J Exp Psychol Hum Percept Perform* **35**, 565–574.
29. Bialystok E, Shapero D (2005) The effect of bilingualism on reversing ambiguous figures. *Dev Sci* **8**, 595–604.
30. Blakemore SJ (2008) The social brain in adolescence. *Nat Rev Neurosci* **9**, 267–277.
31. Block ML, Calderon-Garciduenas L (2009) Air pollution: mechanisms of neuroinflammation and CNS disease. *Trends Neurosci* **32**, 506–516.
32. Bonne O, Grillon C, Vythilingam M *et al.* (2004) Adaptive and maladaptive psychobiological responses to severe psychological stress: implications for the discovery of novel pharmacotherapy. *Neurosci Biobehav Rev* **28**, 65–94.
33. Boyer TW (2006) The development of risk-taking: a multi-perspective review. *Dev Rev* **26**, 291–345.
34. Boyke J, Driemeyer J, Gaser C *et al.* (2008) Training-induced brain structure changes in the elderly. *J Neurosci* **28**, 7031–7035.
35. Bunge SA, Dudukovic NM, Thomason ME *et al.* (2002) Immature frontal lobe contributions to cognitive control in children: evidence from fMRI. *Neuron* **33**, 301–311.
36. Burke CA (2010) Mindfulness-based approaches with children and adolescents: a preliminary review of current research in an emergent field. *J Child Fam Stud* **19**, 133–144.
37. Burnett S, Sebastian C, Cohen Kadosh K *et al.* (2011) The social brain in adolescence: evidence from functional magnetic resonance imaging and behavioural studies. *Neurosci Biobehav Rev* **35**(8), 1654–1664.
38. Buss AH, Plomin R (1984) *Temperament: Early Developing Personality Traits.* Hillsdale: Lawrence Erlbaum Associates.
39. Cacioppo JT, Norris CJ, Decety J *et al.* (2009) In the eye of the beholder: individual differences in perceived social isolation predict regional brain activation to social stimuli. *J. Cognit Neurosci* **21**, 83–92.
40. Canadian_Medical_Association (2008) No Breathing Room: National Illness Costs of Air Pollution. Ottawa, Canada: http://www.cma.ca/index.cfm/ci_id/86830/la_id/1.htm
41. Carr N (2010) *The Shallows: What the Internet Is Doing to Our Brains.* New York: W. W. Norton.
42. Carver CS, Sutton SK, Scheier MF (2000) Action, emotion, and personality: emerging conceptual integration. *Pers Soc Psychol Bull* **26**, 741–751.
43. Casey BJ, Getz S, Galvan A (2008) The adolescent brain. *Dev Rev* **28**, 62–77.
44. Casey BJ, Jones RM, Levita L *et al.* (2010) The storm and stress of adolescence: insights from human imaging and mouse genetics. *Dev Psychobiol* **52**, 225–235.
45. Casey BJ, Trainor R, Giedd J *et al.* (1997) The role of the anterior cingulate in automatic and controlled processes: a developmental neuroanatomical study. *Dev Psychobiol* **30**, 61–69.
46. Caspi A, McClay J, Moffitt TE *et al.* (2002) Role of genotype in the cycle of violence in maltreated children. *Science* **297**, 851–854.
47. Cauffman E, Shulman EP, Steinberg L *et al.* (2010) Age differences in affective decision making as indexed by performance on the Iowa gambling task. *Dev Psychol* **46**, 193–207.
48. Caviness VS, Jr., Kennedy DN, Richelme C *et al.* (1996) The human brain age 7–11 years: a volumetric analysis based on magnetic resonance images. *Cereb Cortex* **6**, 726–736.
49. Chaddock L, Erickson KI, Prakash RS *et al.* (2010) A neuroimaging investigation of the association between aerobic fitness, hippocampal volume, and memory performance in preadolescent children. *Brain Res* **1358**, 172–183.
50. Chaddock L, Erickson KI, Prakash RS *et al.* (2010) Basal ganglia volume is associated with aerobic fitness in preadolescent children. *Dev Neurosci* **32**, 249–256.
51. Chaddock L, Hillman CH, Buck SM *et al.* (2010) Aerobic fitness and executive control of relational memory in preadolescent children. *Med Sci Sports Exerc*.

52. Chein J, Albert D, O'Brien L *et al.* (2011) Peers increase adolescent risk taking by enhancing activity in the brain's reward circuitry. *Dev Sci* **14**, F1–F10.

53. Chiang MC, Barysheva M, Shattuck DW *et al.* (2009) Genetics of brain fiber architecture and intellectual performance. *J Neurosci* **29**, 2212–2224.

54. Chiang MC, McMahon KL, de Zubicaray GI *et al.* (2011) Genetics of white matter development: a DTI study of 705 twins and their siblings aged 12 to 29. *Neuroimage* **54**, 2308–2317.

55. Chiesa A, Serretti A (2010) A systematic review of neurobiological and clinical features of mindfulness meditations. *Eur Psychiatr* **25**, 1044–1044.

56. Christakou A, Brammer M, Rubia K (2011) Maturation of limbic corticostriatal activation and connectivity associated with developmental changes in temporal discounting. *Neuroimage* **54**, 1344–1355.

57. Chrousos GP, Kino T (2007) Glucocorticoid action networks and complex psychiatric and/or somatic disorders. *Stress* **10**, 213–219.

58. Chugani HT (1994) Development of regional brain glucose metabolism in relation to behavior and plasticity. In *Human behavior and the developing brain*, pp. 153–175 [G Dawson, KW Fischer, editors]. New York: Guilford.

59. Chugani HT (1996) Neuroimaging of developmental nonlinearity and developmental pathologies. In *Developmental neuroimaging*, pp. 187–195 [TW Thatcher, GR Lyon, J Rumsey, N Krasnegor, editors]. San Diego: Academic.

60. Ciesielski KT, Knight JE (1994) Cerebellar abnormality in autism: a nonspecific effect of early brain damage? *Acta Neurobiol Exp* **54**, 151–154.

61. Cillessen AHN, Bukowski WM, Haselager GJT (2000) Stability of sociometric categories. *New Dir Child Adolesc Dev* **88**, 75–93.

62. Clark AS, Maclusky NJ, Goldman-Rakic PS (1988) Androgen binding and metabolism in the cerebral cortex of the developing Rhesus monkey. *Endocrinology* **123**, 932–940.

63. Cohen-Kadosh K, Henson RN, Cohen-Kadosh R *et al.* (2010) Task-dependent activation of face-sensitive cortex: an fMRI adaptation study. *J Cognit Neurosci* **22**, 903–917.

64. Conklin HM, Luciana M, Hooper CJ *et al.* (2007) Working memory performance in typically developing children and adolescents: behavioral evidence of protracted frontal lobe development. *Dev Neuropsychol* **31**, 103–128.

65. Crone EA, Bullens L, van der Plas EAA *et al.* (2008) Developmental changes and individual differences in risk and perspective taking in adolescence. *Dev Psychopathol* **20**, 1213–1229.

66. Crone EA, van der Molen MW (2004) Developmental changes in real life decision making: performance on a gambling task previously shown to depend on the ventromedial prefrontal cortex. *Dev Neuropsychol* **25**, 251–279.

67. Crowe SL, Blair RJR (2008) The development of antisocial behavior: what can we learn from functional neuroimaging studies? *Dev Psychopath* **20**, 1145–1159.

68. Csikszentmihalyi M (1990) *Flow: The Psychology of Optimal Experience.* New York: HarperCollins.

69. Cunningham MG, Bhattacharyya S, Benes FM (2002) Amygdalo-cortical sprouting continues into early adulthood: implications for the development of normal and abnormal function during adolescence. *J Comp Neurol* **453**, 116–130.

70. Dahl RE (2004) Adolescent brain development: a period of vulnerabilities and opportunities. Keynote address. *Ann N Y Acad Sci* **1021**, 1–22.

71. Davidson MC, Amso D, Anderson LC *et al.* (2006) Development of cognitive control and executive functions from 4 to 13 years: evidence from manipulations of memory, inhibition, and task switching. *Neuropsychologia* **44**, 2037–2078.

72. Davidson RJ (1998) Affective style and affective disorders: perspectives from affective neuroscience. *Cognit Emot* **12**, 307–330.

73. Davidson RJ, Kabat-Zinn J, Schumacher J *et al.* (2003) Alterations in brain and immune function produced by mindfulness meditation. *Psychosom Med* **65**, 564–570.

74. Davis CL, Tomporowski PD, Boyle CA *et al.* (2007) Effects of aerobic exercise on overweight children's cognitive functioning: a randomized controlled trial. *Res Q Exerc Sport* **78**, 510–519.

75. Davis CL, Tomporowski PD, McDowell JE *et al.* (2011) Exercise improves executive function and achievement and alters brain activation in overweight children: a randomized, controlled trial. *Health Psychol* **30**, 91–98.

76. Decety J (2010) The neurodevelopment of empathy in humans. *Developmental Neuroscience* **32**, 257–267.
77. Decety J, Michalska KJ (2010) Neurodevelopmental changes in the circuits underlying empathy and sympathy from childhood to adulthood. *Dev Sci* **13**, 886–899.
78. Devous MD, Sr., Altuna D, Furl N *et al.* (2006) Maturation of speech and language functional neuroanatomy in pediatric normal controls. *J Speech Lang Hear Res* **49**, 856–866.
79. Doidge N (2007) *The Brain that Changes Itself.* New York: Viking Press.
80. Dosenbach NU, Nardos B, Cohen AL *et al.* (2010) Prediction of individual brain maturity using fMRI. *Science* **329**, 1358–1361.
81. Draganski B, Gaser C, Busch V *et al.* (2004) Neuroplasticity: changes in grey matter induced by training. *Nature* **427**, 311–312.
82. Driemeyer J, Boyke J, Gaser C *et al.* (2008) Changes in gray matter induced by learning-revisited. *PLoS One* **3**, e2669.
83. Dumontheil I, Houlton R, Christoff K *et al.* (2010) Development of relational reasoning during adolescence. *Dev Sci* **13**, F15–24.
84. Dwyer JB, McQuown SC, Leslie FM (2009) The dynamic effects of nicotine on the developing brain. *Pharmacol Therapeut* **122**, 125–139.
85. Eisenberg N (2000) Emotion, regulation, and moral development. *Annu Rev Psychol* **51**, 665–697.
86. Eisenberger NI, Lieberman MD, Williams KD (2003) Does rejection hurt? An FMRI study of social exclusion. *Science* **302**, 290–292.
87. Elbert T, Pantev C, Wienbruch C *et al.* (1995) Increased cortical representation of the fingers of the left hand in string players. *Science* **270**, 305–307.
88. Emery CA, Kang J, Shrier I *et al.* (2010) Risk of injury associated with body checking among youth ice hockey players. *JAMA* **303**, 2265–2272.
89. Ernst M, Fudge JL (2009) A developmental neurobiological model of motivated behavior: anatomy, connectivity and ontogeny of the triadic nodes. *Neurosci Biobehav Rev* **33**, 367–382.
90. Ernst M, Mueller SC (2008) The adolescent brain: insights from functional neuroimaging research. *Dev Neurobiol* **68**, 729–743.
91. Ernst M, Nelson EE, Jazbec S *et al.* (2005) Amygdala and nucleus accumbens in responses to receipt and omission of gains in adults and adolescents. *Neuroimage* **25**, 1279–1291.
92. Fair DA, Cohen AL, Dosenbach NU *et al.* (2008) The maturing architecture of the brain's default network. *Proc Nat Acad Sci U S A* **105**, 4028–4032.
93. Fair DA, Cohen AL, Power JD *et al.* (2009) Functional brain networks develop from a "local to distributed" organization. *PLoS Comput Biol* **5**, e1000381.
94. Farroni T, Csibra G, Simion F *et al.* (2002) Eye contact detection in humans from birth. *Proc Nat Acad Sci U S A* **99**, 9602–9605.
95. Fields RD (2008) Oligodendrocytes changing the rules: action potentials in glia and oligodendrocytes controlling action potentials. *Neuroscientist* **14**, 540–543.
96. Fields RD (2008) White matter in learning, cognition and psychiatric disorders. *Trends Neurosci* **31**, 361–370.
97. Figner B, Mackinlay RJ, Wilkening F *et al.* (2009) Affective and deliberative processes in risky choice: age differences in risk taking in the Columbia card task. *J Exp Psychol Learn Mem Cognit* **35**, 709–730.
98. Froh JJ, Kashdan TB, Yurkewicz C *et al.* (2010) The benefits of passion and absorption in activities: Engaged living in adolescents and its role in psychological well-being. *J Pos Psychol* **5**, 311–332.
99. Fryer SL, Frank LR, Spadoni AD *et al.* (2008) Microstructural integrity of the corpus callosum linked with neuropsychological performance in adolescents. *Brain Cognit* **67**, 225–233.
100. Fujioka T, Ross B, Kakigi R *et al.* (2006) One year of musical training affects development of auditory cortical-evoked fields in young children. *Brain* **129**, 2593–2608.
101. Galvan A, Hare T, Voss H *et al.* (2007) Risk-taking and the adolescent brain: who is at risk? *Dev Sci* **10**, F8–F14.
102. Galvan A, Hare TA, Parra CE *et al.* (2006) Earlier development of the accumbens relative to orbitofrontal cortex might underlie risk-taking behavior in adolescents. *J Neurosci* **26**, 6885–6892.
103. Gardner M, Steinberg L (2005) Peer influence on risk taking, risk preference, and risky decision making in adolescence and adulthood: an experimental study. *Dev Psychol* **41**, 625–635.

104. Geier CF, Terwilliger R, Teslovich T *et al.* (2010) Immaturities in reward processing and its influence on inhibitory control in adolescence. *Cereb Cortex* **20**, 1613–1629.
105. Gentile D (2009) Pathological video-game use among youth ages 8 to 18: a national study. *Psychol Sci* **20**, 594–602.
106. Giedd JN (2002) PBS interview: Inside the Teenage Brain. http://www.pbs.org/wgbh/pages/frontline/shows/teenbrain/interviews/giedd.html.
107. Giedd JN, Blementhal J, Jeffries NO *et al.* (1999) Brain development during childhood and adolescence: a longitudinal MRI study. *Nat Neurosci* **2**, 861–863.
108. Giedd JN, Castellanos FX, Rajapakse JC *et al.* (1997) Sexual dimorphism of the developing human brain. *Progr Neuro Psychopharmacol Biol Psychiatr* **21**, 1185–1201.
109. Giedd JN, Clasen LS, Lenroot R *et al.* (2006) Puberty-related influences on brain development. *Mol Cell Endocrinol* **254–255**, 154–162.
110. Giedd JN, Rapoport JL (2010) Structural MRI of pediatric brain development: what have we learned and where are we going? *Neuron* **67**, 728–734.
111. Giedd JN, Snell JW, Lange N *et al.* (1996) Quantitative magnetic resonance imaging of human brain development: ages 4–18. *Cereb Cortex* **6**, 551–560.
112. Giedd JN, Stockman M, Weddle C *et al.* (2010) Anatomic magnetic resonance imaging of the developing child and adolescent brain and effects of genetic variation. *Neuropsychol Rev* **20**, 349–361.
113. Giorgio A, Watkins KE, Douaud G *et al.* (2008) Changes in white matter microstructure during adolescence. *Neuroimage* **39**, 52–61.
114. Gogtay N, Giedd JN, Lusk L *et al.* (2004) Dynamic mapping of human cortical development during childhood through early adulthood. *Proc Nat Acad Sci U S A* **101**, 8174–8179.
115. Gogtay N, Thompson PM (2010) Mapping gray matter development: implications for typical development and vulnerability to psychopathology. *Brain Cogn* **72**(1), 6–15.
116. Golarai G, Ghahremani DG, Whitfield-Gabrieli S *et al.* (2007) Differential development of high-level visual cortex correlates with category-specific recognition memory. *Nat Neurosci* **10**, 512–522.
117. Goldin PR, Gross JJ (2010) Effects of mindfulness-based stress reduction (MBSR) on emotion regulation in social anxiety disorder. *Emotion* **10**, 83–91.
118. Gray JA (1981) A critique of Eysenck's theory of personality. In *A model for personality*, pp. 246–277 [HJ Eysenck, editor]. Berlin: Springer.
119. Grosbras MH, Jansen M, Leonard G *et al.* (2007) Neural mechanisms of resistance to peer influence in early adolescence. *J Neurosci* **27**, 8040–8045.
120. Guerri C, Pascual M (2010) Mechanisms involved in the neurotoxic, cognitive, and neurobehavioral effects of alcohol consumption during adolescence. *Alcohol* **44**, 15–26.
121. Gunnar MR, Wewerka S, Frenn K *et al.* (2009) Developmental changes in hypothalamus–pituitary–adrenal activity over the transition to adolescence: normative changes and associations with puberty. *Dev Psychopathol* **21**, 69–85.
122. Gur RC, Turetsky BI, Matsui M *et al.* (1999) Sex differences in brain gray and white matter in healthy young adults: correlations with cognitive performance. *J Neurosci* **19**, 4065–4072.
123. Guyer AE, Monk CS, McClure-Tone EB *et al.* (2008) A developmental examination of amygdala response to facial expressions. *J Cognit Neurosci* **20**, 1565–1582.
124. Hackman DA, Farah MJ (2009) Socioeconomic status and the developing brain. *Trends Cognit Sci* **13**, 65–73.
125. Hackman DA, Farah MJ, Meaney MJ (2010) Socioeconomic status and the brain: mechanistic insights from human and animal research. *Nat Rev Neurosci* **11**, 651–659.
126. Hardin MG, Ernst M (2009) Functional brain imaging of development-related risk and vulnerability for substance use in adolescents. *J Addiction Med* **3**, 47–54. 10.1097/ADM.1090b1013e31819ca31788.
127. Hare TA, Tottenham N, Galvan A *et al.* (2008) Biological substrates of emotional reactivity and regulation in adolescence during an emotional go–nogo task. *Biol Psychiatry* **63**, 927–934.
128. Harper LV (2005) Epigenetic inheritance and the intergenerational transfer of experience. *Psychol Bull* **131**, 340–360.
129. Haxby J, Hoffman EA, Gobbini MI (2002) Human neural systems for face recognition and social communication. *Biol Psychiatr* **51**, 59–67.
130. Hayward C, Sanborn K (2002) Puberty and the emergence of gender differences in psychopathology. *J Adolesc Health* **30**, 49–58.

131. Hemphill SA, Kotevski A, Herrenkohl TI *et al.* (2010) Pubertal stage and the prevalence of violence and social/relational aggression. *Pediatrics* **126**, e298–305.
132. Henquet C, Krabbendam L, Spauwen J *et al.* (2005) Prospective cohort study of cannabis use, predisposition for psychosis, and psychotic symptoms in young people. *BMJ* **330**, 11.
133. Herwig U, Kaffenberger T, Jäncke L *et al.* (2010) Self-related awareness and emotion regulation. *Neuroimage* **50**, 734–741.
134. Hikosaka O, Isoda M (2010) Switching from automatic to controlled behavior: cortico-basal ganglia mechanisms. *Trends Cogn Sci* **14**, 154–161.
135. Hillman CH, Castelli DM, Buck SM (2005) Aerobic fitness and neurocognitive function in healthy preadolescent children. *Med Sci Sports Exerc* **37**, 1967–1974.
136. Hofer S, Frahm J (2006) Topography of the human corpus callosum revisited–comprehensive fiber tractography using diffusion tensor magnetic resonance imaging. *Neuroimage* **32**(3), 989–994.
137. Holzel BK, Carmody J, Evans KC *et al.* (2010) Stress reduction correlates with structural changes in the amygdala. *Soc Cogn Affect Neurosci* **5**, 11–17.
138. Holzel BK, Carmody J, Vangel M *et al.* (2011) Mindfulness practice leads to increases in regional brain gray matter density. *Psychiatry Res* **191**, 36–43.
139. Huttenlocher P (1984) Synapse elimination and plasticity in developing human cerebral cortex. *Am J Ment Defic* **88**, 488–496.
140. Hwang K, Velanova K, Luna B (2010) Strengthening of top-down frontal cognitive control networks underlying the development of inhibitory control: a functional magnetic resonance imaging effective connectivity study. *J Neurosci Offi J Soc Neurosci* **30**, 15535–15545.
141. Hyde KL, Lerch J, Norton A *et al.* (2009) Musical training shapes structural brain development. *J Neurosci* **29**, 3019–3025.
142. Imperati D, Colcombe S, Kelly C *et al.* (2011) Differential development of human brain white matter tracts. *PLoS One* **6**, e23437.
143. Irwin CE, Burg SJ, Uhler Cart C (2002) America's adolescents: where have we been, where are we going? *J Adolesc Health* **31**, 91–121.
144. Jazbec S, Hardin M, Schroth E *et al.* (2006) Age-related influence of contingencies on a saccade task. *Exp Brain Res* **174**, 754–762.
145. Johansen-Berg H, Della-Maggiore V, Behrens TE *et al.* (2007) Integrity of white matter in the corpus callosum correlates with bimanual co-ordination skills. *Neuroimage* **36 Suppl 2**, T16–21.
146. Jovanovic H, Perski A, Berglund H *et al.* (2011) Chronic stress is linked to 5-HT1A receptor changes and functional disintegration of the limbic networks. *Neuroimage* **55**, 1178–1188.
147. Jucaite A, Forssberg H, Karlsson P *et al.* (2010) Age-related reduction in dopamine D1 receptors in the human brain: from late childhood to adulthood, a positron emission tomography study. *Neuroscience* **167**, 104–110.
148. Kafouri S, Leonard G, Perron M *et al.* (2009) Maternal cigarette smoking during pregnancy and cognitive performance in adolescence. *Int J Epidemiol* **38**, 158–172.
149. Kahn RS, Khoury J, Nichols WC *et al.* (2003) Role of dopamine transporter genotype and maternal prenatal smoking in childhood hyperactive-impulsive, inattentive, and oppositional behaviors. *J Pediatr* **143**, 104–110.
150. Kamijo K, Pontifex MB, O'Leary KC *et al.* (2011) The effects of an afterschool physical activity program on working memory in preadolescent children. *Dev Sci* **14**, 1046–1058.
151. Karle JW, Watter S, Shedden JM (2010) Task switching in video game players: benefits of selective attention but not resistance to proactive interference. *Acta Psychol (Amst)* **134**, 70–78.
152. Kelly AMC, Di Martino A, Uddin LQ *et al.* (2009) Development of anterior cingulate functional connectivity from late childhood to early adulthood. *Cereb Cortex* **19**, 640–657.
153. Kessler RC, Berglund P, Demler O *et al.* (2005) Lifetime prevalence and age-of-onset distributions of DSM-IV disorders in the national comorbidity survey replication. *Arch Gen Psychiatr* **62**, 593–602.
154. Klump KL, McGue M, Iacono WG (2003) Differential heritability of eating attitudes and behaviors in prepubertal versus pubertal twins. *Int J Eat Disord* **33**, 287–292.
155. Kohls G, Peltzer J, Herpertz-Dahlmann B *et al.* (2009) Differential effects of social and non-social reward on response inhibition in children and adolescents. *Dev Sci* **12**, 614–625.
156. Kramer AF, Erickson KI, Colcombe SJ (2006) Exercise, cognition, and the aging brain. *J Appl Physiol* **101**, 1237–1242.

157. Lang PJ, Bradley MM, Cuthbert BN (1997) Motivated attention: affect, activation, and action. In *Attention and orienting: Sensory and motivational processes*, pp. 97–135 [PJ Lang, RF Simons, MT Balaban, editors]. Mahwah: Erlbaum.

158. Lasky-Su J, Faraone S, Lange C *et al.* (2007) A study of how socioeconomic status moderates the relationship between SNPs encompassing BDNF and ADHD symptom counts in ADHD families. *Behav Genet* **37**, 487–497.

159. Laughlin SB, Sejnowski TJ (2003) Communication in neuronal networks. *Science* **301**, 1870–1874.

160. Lenroot RK, Schmitt JE, Ordaz SJ *et al.* (2009) Differences in genetic and environmental influences on the human cerebral cortex associated with development during childhood and adolescence. *Hum Brain Mapp* **30**, 163–174.

161. Li TQ, Noseworthy MD (2002) Mapping the development of white matter tracts with diffusion tensor imaging. *Dev Sci* **5**, 293–300.

162. Loeber R, Farrington DP, Waschbush DA (1998) Serious and violent juvenile offenders. In *Serious and violent juvenile offenders: Risk factors and successful interventions*, pp. 13–29 [R Loeber, DP Farrington, editors]. Thousand Oaks: Sage.

163. Lotfipour S, Ferguson E, Leonard G *et al.* (2009) Orbitofrontal cortex and drug use during adolescence: role of prenatal exposure to maternal smoking and BDNF genotype. *Arch Gen Psychiatr* **66**, 1244–1252.

164. Lövdén M, Bäckman L, Lindenberger U *et al.* (2010) A theoretical framework for the study of adult cognitive plasticity. *Psychol Bull* **136**, 659–676.

165. Lu LH, Sowell ER (2009) Morphological development of the brain: what imaging has told us. In *Neuroimaging in developmental clinical neuroscience* [Rumsey JM, Ernst M, editors]. Boston: Cambridge University Press.

166. Lu L, Leonard C, Thompson P *et al.* (2007) Normal developmental changes in inferior frontal gray matter are associated with improvement in phonological processing: a longitudinal MRI analysis. *Cereb Cortex* **17**, 1092–1099.

167. Lubman DI, Yucel M, Lawrence AJ (2008) Inhalant abuse among adolescents: neurobiological considerations. *Br J Pharmacol* **154**, 316–326.

168. Luders E, Thompson PM, Narr KL *et al.* (2011) The link between callosal thickness and intelligence in healthy children and adolescents. *Neuroimage* **54**, 1823–1830.

169. Luna B (2009) Developmental changes in cognitive control through adolescence. In *Advances in child development and behavior*, pp. 233–278 [B Patricia, editor]. Greenwich, CT.

170. Luna B, Padmanabhan A, O'Hearn K (2010) What has fMRI told us about the development of cognitive control through adolescence? *Brain Cogn* **72**, 101–113.

171. Luna B, Sweeney JA (2004) The emergence of collaborative brain function: FMRI studies of the development of response inhibition. *Ann N Y Acad Sci* **1021**, 296–309.

172. Mabbott DJ, Rovet J, Noseworthy MD *et al.* (2009) The relations between white matter and declarative memory in older children and adolescents. *Brain Res* **1294**, 80–90.

173. Madsen KS, Baare WF, Vestergaard M *et al.* (2010) Response inhibition is associated with white matter microstructure in children. *Neuropsychologia* **48**, 854–862.

174. Manuck SB, Flory JD, Ferrell RE *et al.* (2004) Socio-economic status covaries with central nervous system serotonergic responsivity as a function of allelic variation in the serotonin transporter gene-linked polymorphic region. *Psychoneuroendocrinology* **29**, 651–668.

175. Maslach C (2001) What have we learned about burnout and health? *Psychol Health* **16**, 607–611.

176. Masten AS (2001) Ordinary magic: resilience processes in development. *Am Psychol* **56**, 227–238.

177. McCormick CM, Mathews IZ, Thomas C *et al.* (2010) Investigations of HPA function and the enduring consequences of stressors in adolescence in animal models. *Brain Cogn* **72**, 73–85.

178. McCormick CM, Thomas CM, Sheridan CS *et al.* (2011) Social instability stress in adolescent male rats alters hippocampal neurogenesis and produces deficits in spatial location memory in adulthood. *Hippocampus* **22**(6), 1300–1312.

179. McCrory E, De Brito SA, Viding E (2010) Research review: the neurobiology and genetics of maltreatment and adversity. *J Child Psychol Psychiatr Allied Disciplines* **51**, 1079–1095.

180. McDougall P, Hymel S, Vaillancourt T *et al.* (2001) The consequences of childhood rejection. In *Interpersonal rejection*, pp. 213–247 [MR Leary, editor]. New York: Oxford University Press.

181. McQueeny T, Schweinsburg BC, Schweinsburg AD *et al.* (2009) Altered white matter integrity in adolescent binge drinkers. *Alcohol Clin Exp Res* **33**, 1278–1285.

182. Meyer-Lindenberg A, Buckholtz JW, Kolachana B *et al.* (2006) Neural mechanisms of genetic risk for impulsivity and violence in humans. *Proc Natl Acad Sci U S A* **103**(16), 6269–6274.
183. Mitra R, Jadhav S, McEwen BS *et al.* (2005) Stress duration modulates the spatiotemporal patterns of spine formation in the basolateral amygdala. *Proc Nat Acad Sci U S A* **102**, 9371–9376.
184. Monk CS, McClure EB, Nelson EE *et al.* (2003) Adolescent immaturity in attention-related brain engagement to emotional facial expressions. *Neuroimage* **20**, 420–428.
185. Morse JK, Scheff SW, DeKosky ST (1986) Gonadal steroids influence axon sprouting in the hippocampal dentate gyrus: a sexually dimorphic response. *Exp Neurol* **94**, 649–658.
186. Morton JB, Harper SN (2007) What did Simon say? Revisiting the bilingual advantage. *Dev Sci* **10**, 719–726.
187. Mueller EM, Hofmann SG, Santesso DL *et al.* (2009) Electrophysiological evidence of attentional biases in social anxiety disorder. *Psychol Med* **39**, 1141–1152.
188. Nagel BJ, Medina KL, Yoshii J *et al.* (2006) Age-related changes in prefrontal white matter volume across adolescence. *Neuroreport* **17**, 1427–1431.
189. Nagy Z, Westerberg H, Klingberg T (2004) Maturation of white matter is associated with the development of cognitive functions during childhood. *J Cogn Neurosci* **16**, 1227–1233.
190. Nelson EE, Leibenluft E, McClure EB *et al.* (2005) The social re-orientation of adolescence: a neuroscience perspective on the process and its relation to psychopathology. *Psychol Med* **35**, 163–174.
191. Neuman RJ, Lobos E, Reich W *et al.* (2007) Prenatal smoking exposure and dopaminergic genotypes interact to cause a severe ADHD subtype. *Biol Psychiatr* **61**, 1320–1328.
192. O'Leary-Moore SK, Galloway MP, McMechan AP *et al.* (2009) Neurochemical changes after acute binge toluene inhalation in adolescent and adult rats: a high-resolution magnetic resonance spectroscopy study. *Neurotoxicol Teratol* **31**, 382–389.
193. Olson IR, Plotzker A, Ezzyat Y (2007) The Enigmatic temporal pole: a review of findings on social and emotional processing. *Brain* **130**, 1718–1731.
194. Ophir E, Nass C, Wagner AD (2009) Cognitive control in media multitaskers. *Proc Nat Acad Sci U S A* **106**, 15583–15587.
195. Ostby Y, Tamnes CK, Fjell AM *et al.* (2009) Heterogeneity in subcortical brain development: a structural magnetic resonance imaging study of brain maturation from 8 to 30 years. *J Neurosci* **29**, 11772–11782.
196. Page AS, Cooper AR, Griew P *et al.* (2010) Children's screen viewing is related to psychological difficulties irrespective of physical activity. *Pediatrics* **126**, e1011–e1017.
197. Pantev C, Oostenveld R, Engelien A *et al.* (1998) Increased auditory cortical representation in musicians. *Nature* **392**, 811–814.
198. Pantev C, Roberts LE, Schulz M *et al.* (2001) Timbre-specific enhancement of auditory cortical representations in musicians. *Neuroreport* **12**, 169–174.
199. Patton GC, Hibbert ME, Carlin J *et al.* (1996) Menarche and the onset of depression and anxiety in Victoria, Australia. *J Epidemiol Community Health* **50**, 661–666.
200. Patton GC, McMorris BJ, Toumbourou JW *et al.* (2004) Puberty and the onset of substance use and abuse. *Pediatrics* **114**, e300–306.
201. Paus T, Collins DL, Evans AC *et al.* (2001) Maturation of white matter in the human brain: a review of magnetic resonance studies. *Brain Res Bull* **54**, 255–266.
202. Paus T, Nawaz-Khan I, Leonard G *et al.* (2010) Sexual dimorphism in the adolescent brain: role of testosterone and androgen receptor in global and local volumes of grey and white matter. *Horm Behav* **57**, 63–75.
203. Paus T, Nawazkhan I, Leonard G *et al.* (2008) Corpus callosum in adolescent offspring exposed prenatally to maternal cigarette smoking. *Neuroimage* **40**, 435–441.
204. Peper JS, Brouwer RM, Schnack HG *et al.* (2009) Sex steroids and brain structure in pubertal boys and girls. *Psychoneuroendocrinology* **34**, 332–342.
205. Peper JS, Brouwer RM, Schnack HG *et al.* (2008) Cerebral white matter in early puberty is associated with luteinizing hormone concentrations. *Psychoneuroendocrinology* **33**, 909–915.
206. Perrin JS, Herve P-Y, Leonard G *et al.* (2008) Growth of white matter in the adolescent brain: role of testosterone and androgen receptor. *J Neurosci* **28**, 9519–9524.
207. Pessoa L, Engelmann JB (2010) Embedding reward signals into perception and cognition. *Front Neurosci* **5**, 5.

208. Pollak SD, Cicchetti D, Hornung K *et al.* (2000) Recognizing emotion in faces: developmental effects of child abuse and neglect. *Dev Psychol* **36**, 679–688.
209. Pollak SD, Klorman R, Thatcher JE, Cicchetti D (2001) P3b reflects maltreated children's reactions to facial displays of emotion. *Psychophysiology* **38**, 267–274.
210. Pollak SD, Messner M, Kistler DJ *et al.* (2009) Development of perceptual expertise in emotion recognition. *Cognition* **110**, 242–247.
211. Pollak SD, Tolley-Schell SA (2003) Selective attention to facial emotion in physically abused children. *J Abnorm Psychol* **112**, 323–338.
212. Qiu J, Li H, Wei Y *et al.* (2008) Neural mechanisms underlying the processing of Chinese and English words in a word generation task: an event-related potential study. *Psychophysiology* **45**, 970–976.
213. Quevedo KM, Benning SD, Gunnar MR *et al.* (2009) The onset of puberty: effects on the psychophysiology of defensive and appetitive motivation. *Dev Psychopathol* **21**, 27–45.
214. Raichle ME (2010) Two views of brain function. *Trends Cognit Sci* **14**, 180–190.
215. Raizada RDS, Kishiyama MM (2010) Effects of socioeconomic status on brain development, and how cognitive neuroscience may contribute to levelling the playing field. *Front Hum Neurosci* **4**, 3.
216. Rakic P, Bourgeois J-P, Goldman-Rakic PS (1994) Synaptic development of the cerebral cortex: implications for learning, memory, and mental illness. In *Progress in brain research*, Vol. 102, pp. 227–243 [MA Corner, HBM Uylings, J Van Pelt, FHL da Silva, editors]. Amsterdam: Elsevier.
217. Reiss AL, Abrams MT, Singer HS *et al.* (1996) Brain development, gender and IQ in children. A volumetric imaging study. *Brain* **119**, 1763–1774.
218. Reyna VF, Farley F (2006) Risk and rationality in adolescent decision making: implications for theory, practice, and public policy. *Psychol Sci Publ Interest* **7**, 1–44.
219. Rothbart MK, Bates JE (1998) Temperament. In *Handbook of child psychology*, pp. 108–176 [W Damon, editor]. New York: John Wiley.
220. Rubia K (2009) The neurobiology of meditation and its clinical effectiveness in psychiatric disorders. *Biol Psychol* **82**, 1–11.
221. Rubia K, Overmeyer S, Taylor E *et al.* (2000) Functional frontalisation with age: mapping neurodevelopmental trajectories with fMRI. *Neurosci Biobehav Rev* **24**, 13–19.
222. Sale A, Berardi N, Maffei L (2009) Enrich the environment to empower the brain. *Trends Neurosci* **32**, 233–239.
223. Schellenberg EG (2004) Music lessons enhance IQ. *Psychol Sci* **15**, 511–514.
224. Scherf KS, Behrmann M, Humphreys K *et al.* (2007) Visual category-selectivity for faces, places and objects emerges along different developmental trajectories. *Dev Sci* **10**, F15–F30.
225. Schmidt LA, Jetha MK (2009) Temperament and affect vulnerability: behavioral, electrocortical, and neuroimaging perspectives. In *Handbook of developmental social neuroscience*, pp. 305–323 [M de Haan, MR Gunnar, editors]. New York: Guilford.
226. Schmithorst VJ, Holland SK, Dardzinski BJ (2008) Developmental differences in white matter architecture between boys and girls. *Hum Brain Mapp* **29**, 696–710.
227. Schmithorst VJ, Wilke M, Dardzinski BJ *et al.* (2005) Cognitive functions correlate with white matter architecture in a normal pediatric population: a diffusion tensor MRI study. *Hum Brain Mapp* **26**, 139–147.
228. Scholz J, Klein MC, Behrens TE *et al.* (2009) Training induces changes in white-matter architecture. *Nat Neurosci* **12**, 1370–1371.
229. Sebastian C, Viding E, Williams KD *et al.* (2010) Social brain development and the affective consequences of ostracism in adolescence. *Brain Cogn* **72**, 134–145.
230. Sebastian CL, Tan GC, Roiser JP *et al.* (2011) Developmental influences on the neural bases of responses to social rejection: implications of social neuroscience for education. *Neuroimage* **57**(3), 686–694.
231. Segalowitz SJ, Santesso DL, Willoughby T *et al.* (2012) Adolescent peer interaction and trait surgency weaken medial prefrontal cortex responses to failure. *Soc Cognit Affect Neurosci* **7**(1), 115–124.
232. Shamosh NA, Gray JR (2008) Delay discounting and intelligence: a meta-analysis. *Intelligence* **36**, 289–305.
233. Shaw P, Greenstein D, Lerch J *et al.* (2006) Intellectual ability and cortical development in children and adolescents. *Nature* **440**, 676–679.
234. Shaw P, Kabani NJ, Lerch JP *et al.* (2008) Neurodevelopmental trajectories of the human cerebral cortex. *J Neurosci* **28**, 3586–3594.

235. Sibley BA, Etnier JL (2003) The relationship between physical activity and cognition in children: a meta-analysis. *Pediatr Exerc Sci* **15**, 243–256.
236. Simons-Morton B, Lerner N, Singer J (2005) The observed effects of teenage passengers on the risky driving behavior of teenage drivers. *Accid Anal Prev* **37**, 973–982.
237. Snook L, Paulson LA, Roy D *et al.* (2005) Diffusion tensor imaging of neurodevelopment in children and young adults. *Neuroimage* **26**, 1164–1173.
238. Soliman F, Glatt CE, Bath KG *et al.* (2010) A genetic variant BDNF polymorphism alters extinction learning in both mouse and human. *Science* **327**, 863–866.
239. Somerville LH, Jones RM, Casey BJ (2010) A time of change: behavioral and neural correlates of adolescent sensitivity to appetitive and aversive environmental cues. *Brain Cogn* **72**, 124–133.
240. Sowell ER, Thompson PM, Holmes CJ *et al.* (1999) In vivo evidence for post-adolescent brain maturation in frontal and striatal regions. *Nat Neurosci* **2**, 859–861.
241. Sowell ER, Thompson PM, Tessner KD *et al.* (2001) Mapping continued brain growth and gray matter density reduction in dorsal frontal cortex: inverse relationships during postadolescent brain maturation. *J Neurosci* **21**, 8819–8829.
242. Sowell ER, Thompson PM, Toga AW (2004) Mapping changes in the human cortex throughout the span of life. *Neuroscientist* **10**, 372–392.
243. Sowell ER, Trauner DA, Gamst A *et al.* (2002) Development of cortical and subcortical brain structures in childhood and adolescence: a structural MRI study. *Dev Med Child Neurol* **44**, 4–16.
244. Spear LP (2000) Neurobehavioral changes in adolescence. *Curr Dir Psychol Sci* **9**, 111–114.
245. Spear LP (2009) Heightened stress responsivity and emotional reactivity during pubertal maturation: implications for psychopathology. *Dev Psychopathol* **21**, 87–97.
246. Spear LP (2010) *The Behavioral Neuroscience of Adolescence*. New York: Norton.
247. Stead JD, Neal C, Meng F *et al.* (2006) Transcriptional profiling of the developing rat brain reveals that the most dramatic regional differentiation in gene expression occurs postpartum. *J Neurosci* **26**, 345–353.
248. Steinberg L (2004) Risk taking in adolescence: what changes, and why? *Ann N Y Acad Sci* **1021**, 51–58.
249. Steinberg L (2008) A social neuroscience perspective on adolescent risk-taking. *Dev Rev* **28**, 78–106.
250. Steinberg L (2009) Should the science of adolescent brain development inform public policy? *Am Psychol* **64**, 739–750.
251. Steinberg L, Cauffman E, Woolard J *et al.* (2009) Are adolescents less mature than adults?: minors' access to abortion, the juvenile death penalty, and the alleged APA "flip-flop". *Am Psychol* **64**, 583–594.
252. Steinberg L, Graham S, O'Brien L *et al.* (2009) Age differences in future orientation and delay discounting. *Development* **80**, 28–44.
253. Steinberg L, Monahan KC (2007) Age differences in resistance to peer influence. *Dev Psychol* **43**, 1531–1543.
254. Steinberg L, Scott ES (2003) Less guilty by reason of adolescence: developmental immaturity, diminished responsibility, and the juvenile death penalty. *Am Psychol* **58**, 1009–1018.
255. Stevens MC, Skudlarski P, Pearlson GD *et al.* (2009) Age-related cognitive gains are mediated by the effects of white matter development on brain network integration. *Neuroimage* **48**, 738–746.
256. Strenziok M, Krueger F, Deshpande G *et al.* (2010) Fronto-parietal regulation of media violence exposure in adolescents: a multi-method study. *Soc Cognit Affect Neurosci*.
257. Stroud LR, Foster E, Papandonatos GD *et al.* (2009) Stress response and the adolescent transition: performance versus peer rejection stressors. *Dev Psychopathol* **21**, 47–68.
258. Supekar K, Musen M, Menon V (2009) Development of large-scale functional brain networks in children. *PLoS Biol* **7**, e1000157.
259. Takeuchi H, Sekiguchi A, Taki Y *et al.* (2010) Training of working memory impacts structural connectivity. *J Neurosci* **30**, 3297–3303.
260. Tamnes CK, Østby Y, Fjell AM *et al.* (2010) Brain maturation in adolescence and young adulthood: regional age-related changes in cortical thickness and white matter volume and microstructure. *Cerebr Cortex* **20**, 534–548.
261. Tang YY, Ma Y, Wang J *et al.* (2007) Short-term meditation training improves attention and self-regulation. *Proc Natl Acad Sci U S A* **104**, 17152–17156.

262. Tau GZ, Peterson BS (2010) Normal development of brain circuits. *Neuropsychopharmacology* **35**, 147–168.
263. Taylor SE, Way BM, Welch WT *et al.* (2006) Early family environment, current adversity, the serotonin transporter promoter polymorphism, and depressive symptomatology. *Biol Psychiatr* **60**, 671–676.
264. Teicher MH, Barber NI, Gelbard HA *et al.* (1993) Developmental differences in acute nigrostriatal and mesocorticolimbic system response to haloperidol. *Neuropsychopharmacology* **9**, 147–156.
265. Teicher MH, Dumont NL, Ito Y *et al.* (2004) Childhood neglect is associated with reduced corpus callosum area. *Biol Psychiatr* **56**, 80–85.
266. Tiemeier H, Lenroot RK, Greenstein DK *et al.* (2010) Cerebellum development during childhood and adolescence: a longitudinal morphometric MRI study. *Neuroimage* **49**, 63–70.
267. Toro R, Leonard G, Lerner JV *et al.* (2008) Prenatal exposure to maternal cigarette smoking and the adolescent cerebral cortex. *Neuropsychopharmacology* **33**, 1019–1027.
268. Trudeau F, Shephard RJ (2010) Relationships of physical activity to brain health and the academic performance of schoolchildren. *Am J Lifestyle Med* **4**, 138–150.
269. Turkheimer E, Haley A, Waldron M *et al.* (2003) Socioeconomic status modifies heritability of IQ in young children. *Psychol Sci* **14**, 623–628.
270. Uddin LQ, Supekar K, Menon V (2010) Typical and atypical development of functional human brain networks: insights from resting-state FMRI. *Front Syst Neurosci* **4**, 21.
271. Van Leijenhorst L, Westenberg PM, Crone EA (2008) A developmental study of risky decisions on the cake gambling task: age and gender analyses of probability estimation and reward evaluation. *Dev Neuropsychol* **33**, 179–196.
272. Vyas A, Mitra R, Shankaranarayana Rao BS *et al.* (2002) Chronic stress induces contrasting patterns of dendritic remodeling in hippocampal and amygdaloid neurons. *J Neurosci* **22**, 6810–6818.
273. Wahlstrom D, Collins P, White T *et al.* (2010) Developmental changes in dopamine neurotransmission in adolescence: behavioral implications and issues in assessment. *Brain Cogn* **72**, 146–159.
274. Wahlstrom D, White T, Hooper CJ *et al.* (2007) Variations in the catechol O-methyltransferase polymorphism and prefrontally guided behaviors in adolescents. *Biol Psychiatr* **61**, 626–632.
275. Wahlstrom D, White T, Luciana M (2010) Neurobehavioral evidence for changes in dopamine system activity during adolescence. *Neurosci Biobehav Rev* **34**, 631–648.
276. Walhovd KB, Fjell AM, Reinvang I *et al.* (2005) Effects of age on volumes of cortex, white matter and subcortical structures. *Neurobiol Aging* **26**, 1261–1270; discussion 1268–1275.
277. Walker EF, McMillan A, Mittal V (2007) Chapter 12. Neurohormones, neurodevelopment, and the prodrome of psychosis in adolescence. In *Adolescent psychopathology and the developing brain*, pp. 264–284 [DW Romer, F Elaine, editors]. New York: Oxford University Press.
278. Wang Y, Mathews VP, Kalnin AJ *et al.* (2009) Short term exposure to a violent video game induces changes in frontolimbic circuitry in adolescents. *Brain Imaging Behav* **3**, 38–50.
279. Whittle S, Yucel M, Fornito A *et al.* (2008) Neuroanatomical correlates of temperament in early adolescents. *J Am Acad Child Adolesc Psychiatry* **47**, 682–693.
280. Wilke M, Krägeloh-Mann I, Holland S (2007) Global and local development of gray and white matter volume in normal children and adolescents. *Exp Brain Res* **178**, 296–307.
281. Zehle S, Bock J, Jezierski G *et al.* (2007) Methylphenidate treatment recovers stress-induced elevated dendritic spine densities in the rodent dorsal anterior cingulate cortex. *Dev Neurobiol* **67**, 1891–1900.
282. Zehr JL, Todd BJ, Schulz KM *et al.* (2006) Dendritic pruning of the medial amygdala during pubertal development of the male Syrian hamster. *J Neurobiol* **66**, 578–590.
283. Zimring GE (1998) *American Youth Violence*. New York: Oxford University Press.
284. Zoladz JA, Pilc A (2010) The effect of physical activity on the brain derived neurotrophic factor: from animal to human studies. *J Physiol Pharmacol* **61**, 533–541.

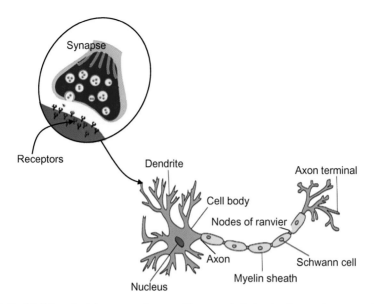

Plate 1 *Fig. 1.1. Schematic of the neuron and synapse. The synapse is the junction that permits one neuron's axon to pass a signal to the receiving neuron's dendrite.*

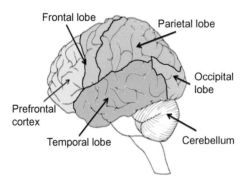

Plate 2 *Fig. 1.2. Schematic of the lateral surface of the brain. The surface gray matter of the lobes comprises the cortex, consisting of the four lobes, with the prefrontal subdivision of the frontal lobe colored in light yellow. The cerebellum is considered to be one of many subcortical structures (i.e., gray matter below the cortex).*

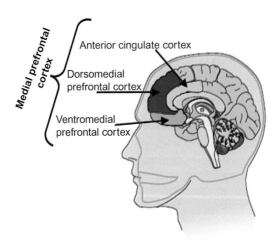

Plate 3 *Fig. 1.3. Schematic of the medial (inside) view of the brain. This view shows the divisions of the medial prefrontal cortex and the anterior cingulate.*

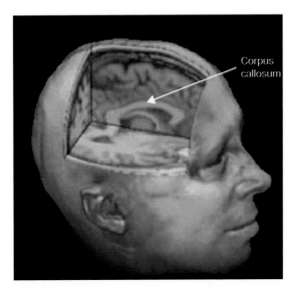

Plate 4 *Fig. 1.4. The corpus callosum is the largest structure of axonal tracts in the brain (approximately 200 million nerve fibers), facilitating interhemispheric communication and influencing language learning and associative thinking. The area of the corpus callosum increases robustly from ages 4 to 22 years. (Source: See Ref. 9.)*

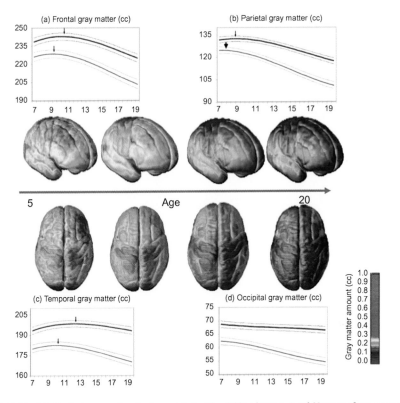

Plate 5 *Fig. 1.5. Cortical gray matter development in healthy children between 4 and 22 years of age rescanned every 2 years. The brain images are of the right lateral and top views showing thickening and thinning of gray matter over maturation. Cortical gray matter appears to progress in a "back-to-front" manner. The color bar indicates the amount of gray matter (red-pink: more grey matter; blue-purple: gray matter loss). The graphs show total lobar volumes in male (blue) and female (red) healthy children aged 7 to 20 years. Arrows indicate peak gray matter volume for each curve, and dotted lines represent the confidence intervals. (Source: See Ref. 115.)*

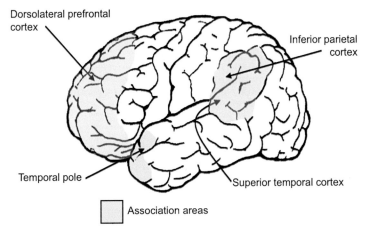

Plate 6 *Fig. 1.6. Association cortex regions with specific subregions labeled. The association areas integrate information from multiple brain regions.*

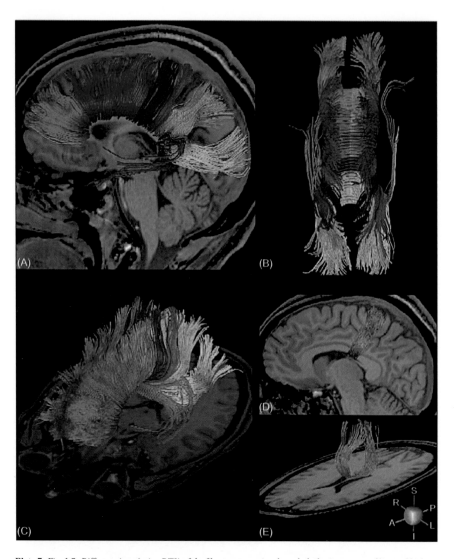

Plate 7 *Fig. 1.7. Different views (using DTI) of the fiber tracts running through the brain as a sort of 'internal highway system' of the cortex. All fibers here connect the hemispheres through the corpus callosum, and then turn upward on both sides. (A) Side view, showing fibers sweeping upward in the medial side of the right hemisphere, in prefrontal (green), premotor (light blue), motor (dark blue), parietal (orange), and occipital (yellow) cortex, and between the left and right temporal lobes (violet). (B) The view of the fibers from front (green) to back (yellow). (C) The side view seen from the top. (D) and (E) Two more views of callosal fibers projecting into primary motor cortex. (Source: See Ref. 136.)*

(I) Mature by adolescence

Association tracts

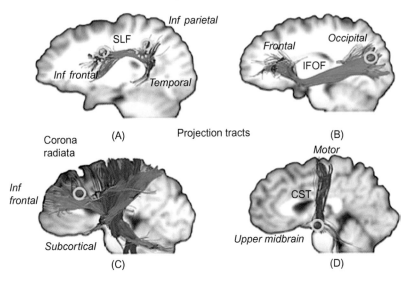

(A)

Projection tracts

(B)

(C)

(D)

(II) Still immature during adolescence

Association tracts

Interhemispheric tract

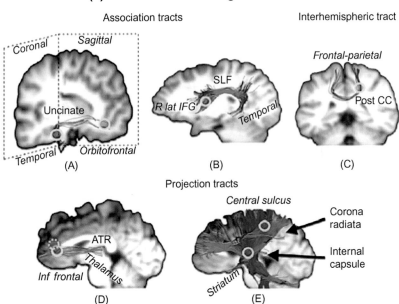

(A)

(B)

(C)

Projection tracts

(D)

(E)

Plate 8 *Fig. 1.8. (I) White matter tracts that are mature by ages 8–12. These are broadly distributed neural networks. (II) White matter tracts that are still maturing in 13–17 year olds. Some of these support top-down executive control over behavior, and some integrate information by communicating between the two hemispheres.* (Source: See Ref. 7, reproduced with permission.)

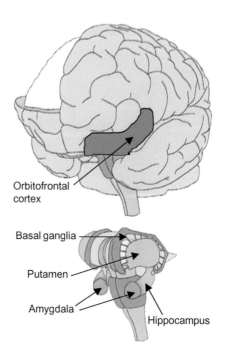

Orbitofrontal cortex

Basal ganglia

Putamen

Amygdala

Hippocampus

Plate 9 *Fig. 1.9. An illustration of how subcortical regions, including the basal ganglia, putamen, amygdala, and hippocampus are tucked inside the cerebral hemispheres. (Source: See Ref. 9.)*

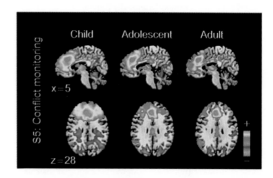

Plate 10 *Fig. 2.1. The cortical connections over childhood (8–12 years) through adolescence (13–17 years), and young adulthood (19–24 years) change from being more diffuse to more focused. (Source: See Ref. 152, reprinted with permission from Oxford University Press.)*

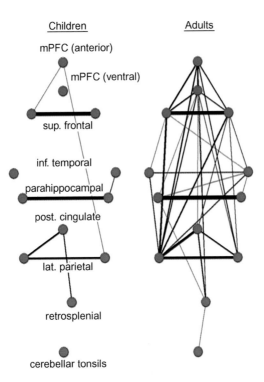

Children   Adults

mPFC (anterior)

mPFC (ventral)

sup. frontal

inf. temporal

parahippocampal

post. cingulate

lat. parietal

retrosplenial

cerebellar tonsils

Plate 11 *Fig. 2.2. From childhood (7–9 years) to adulthood (21–31 years), we see dramatic increases in long-range connections between regions.* (*Source:* Reprinted with permission from Fair et al., 2008. Copyright (2008) National Academy of Sciences, USA.)

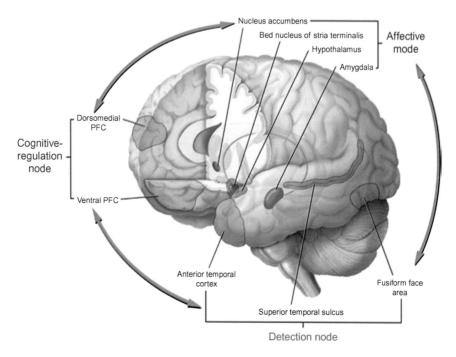

Nucleus accumbens

Bed nucleus of stria terminalis

Hypothalamus

Amygdala

Affective mode

Dorsomedial PFC

Cognitive-regulation node

Ventral PFC

Anterior temporal cortex

Fusiform face area

Superior temporal sulcus

Detection node

Plate 12 *Fig. 3.1. Brain regions that make up the detection node (highlighted in green) are responsible for carrying out the basic perceptual processes of social stimuli. Brain regions that make up the affective node (highlighted in red) interact with the detection node to attach emotional significance to the stimuli. Brain regions that make up the cognitive-regulatory node (highlighted in blue) are involved in controlling response tendencies and understanding others' perspectives. (Source*: Reproduced with permission from Ref. 190.)

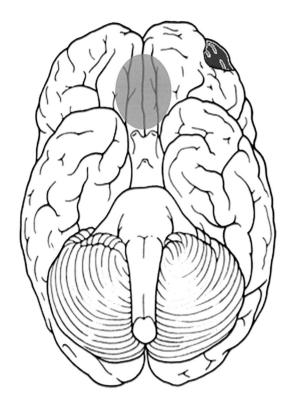

Plate 13 *Fig. 3.3. The areas of the frontal cortex active during empathic responses change from the ventromedial portion (in orange) of the orbitofrontal cortex (OFC) in childhood to the lateral OFC (colored blue) in adulthood, with a gradual shift from 10 to 40 years. (Source: See Ref. 77 for original data.)*

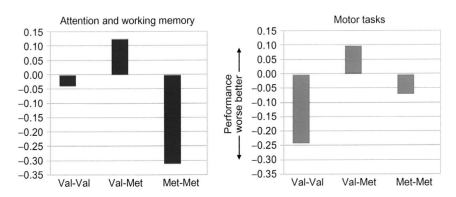

Plate 14 *Fig. 4.2. Neuropsychological performance pattern of dopamine gene combinations (Val vs Met) in adolescence (9–17 years). The Val-Met combination outperforms the other variants on both cognitive and motor tasks during this age period. (Source: Data from Ref. 274.)*

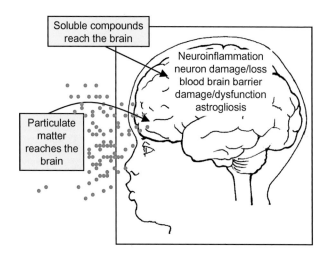

Plate 15 *Fig. 4.4. Air pollution containing fine particulate matter with particles smaller than 2.5 μm (PM2.5) can penetrate into the exchange of gas in the lungs. Some research suggests that these small particles are capable of crossing the blood-brain barrier, leading to inflammation and damage in the brain (Source: See Ref. 31.)*

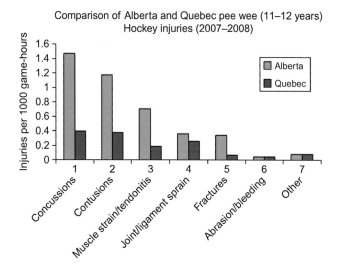

Plate 16 *Fig. 4.5. A comparison of injuries incurred during pee-wee hockey games when cross-checking is allowed (Alberta) versus not allowed (Quebec). (Source: Data from Ref. 88.)*

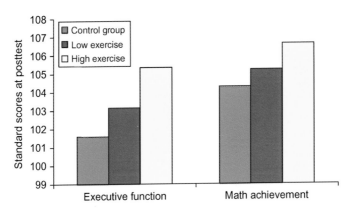

Plate 17 *Fig. 4.6. The effects on executive function and math achievement of a 13-week after-school low (20 min per day) and high (40 min per day) aerobic exercise program for 7–11-year-olds. (Source: Data from Ref. 74.)*

Edwards Brothers Malloy
Ann Arbor MI. USA
February 1, 2013